Friends Are for Helping

Donna Maples

Woman's Missionary Union
Birmingham, Alabama
1982

Ann Kilner, Editor
Kathryne Solomon, Editorial Assistant
Charlotte Harmon, Typesetter
Richard F. Bodenhamer, Artist

Published by Woman's Missionary Union, Auxiliary to Southern Baptist Convention, 600 North 20th Street, Birmingham, Alabama 35203-2680: Dorothy Elliott Sample, President; Carolyn Weatherford, Executive Director; Bobbie Sorrill, Education Division Director; Gertrude A. Tharpe, Editorial Department Director.

Unless otherwise noted, Scripture quotations are from the New American Standard Bible, © The Lockman Foundation 1960, 1962, 1963, 1968, 1971, 1972, 1973, 1975, and 1977. Used by permission.
Good News Bible, Today's English Version (TEV): Used by permission, American Bible Society.
Holy Bible: New International Version, (NIV), © 1978 by New York International Bible Society. Used by permission of Zondervan Bible Publishers.

Photo Credits
All photos from the Home Mission Board: pp. 8, 26, 30, 33, 41, 55, 71, David Clanton; pp. 12, 53, 76, Everett Hullum; pp. 14, 22, 38, Ken Touchton; p. 36, Karen Mitchell; pp. 45, 56, 66, Paul Obregon; pp. 48, 64, 74, 82, Mark Sandlin; pp. 58, 78, Wayne Grimstead; p. 62, Jim Wright.

15M-82

Foreword

A friend is one to whom
   One can pour out all the contents
   of one's heart,
Chaff and grain together,
   Knowing that the gentlest of hands
Will take and sift it
   Keep what is worth keeping
And with the breath of kindness,
   Blow the rest away.

Ancient proverb

F riendship is a miracle really—but it's not one of those split-
second miracles that seem just to happen. It's a miracle built
on hard work. Friendships are made of risks, commitments, com-
promises, caring, hurting, forgiving, communicating, growing, and
living. Many real friendships take years to develop completely, and
yet it is in the process of becoming that friendship brings its
greatest joy.

To take the risk of being a friend, you have to believe in yourself
and in the joy you have inside. You can believe, even in the hard
times, if Christ lives within you. Your joy comes from him, and if
you dare to let people see the real you, you can share this joy with
them. You don't have to be perfect. You don't even have to have

it all together. It's just that since God has given you so much, you have something special to share with others.

Friends are learning to be equal. No one can give all the time, and no one can receive all the time. You don't expect a friend to share his dreams with you if you won't take the risk of sharing yours. You don't dump your problems on a friend and laugh off his problems when he brings them to you. You don't hurt a friend if you can help it. You don't tell your friend's secrets or belittle his hopes and fears. You listen—really listen to a friend. Sometimes you speak, but not too much. You're loyal to a friend. You don't take him for granted and assume he'll be there whenever you need him even though you neglect him in favor of others. You give your friend part of yourself and you don't take it back every time you and your friend disagree. You have your differences—you may even fight—but you're still friends.

You can't possess a friend. You don't expect to take all your friend's time or to make his decisions for him. You let your friend be himself, and he lets you be you. That means the two of you are different. He won't always live up to your expectations. Sometimes this hurts, and you may wish you'd never met. But don't give up. Tell him how you feel, and talk about it. Even angry words spoken by a real friend are better than no communication at all. After the anger comes forgiveness. Friendships survive because friends can forgive. We can forgive because in Christ we are forgiven.

A friend is a person you can share all your feelings with—the good ones, the not-so-good ones, and even the awful ones. A friend is one of the few people you don't have to wear a mask with. You can let your friend see you like you are because you and your friend are helping each other grow toward what you can become. Do you have a friend like this? Maybe you even have two or three. You are fortunate indeed. During an entire lifetime most people experience only a few friendships that reach this level. Everyone wants to have this kind of friend. It's just as important to become this kind of friend. As you read *Friends Are for Helping* you will discover what is involved in friendship on this level—the risks, the commitment, the joys. You will discover new ways to help your friends with their special needs, and you will find opportunities to share your faith in Christ through your helping. Most people would probably agree with the general statement that friendship is worth the cost. As you read this book, consider the more personal question, Is friendship worth the cost FOR YOU? If you decide in favor of friendship, you will find in this book a lot of help for. developing friendships in the midst of day-to-day reality. You will find you can share all that you have received if you're willing to be a friend.

Preface

My friends and I have experienced many special joys as we have helped each other through the high and low spots of our lives. We have cried together, laughed together, and struggled together as we have searched out answers to questions and found new directions for our lives. Our relationships have been strengthened as we have learned to lean on each other and to steady each other.

My hope in writing this book is that you will grow in your ability to help your friends and to be helped by them. As a Christian, you will discover new opportunities to witness through helping experiences with friends who are not Christians. This book offers guidelines for making friends, learning to trust each other, and offering the special kinds of help which friends are uniquely able to give.

I would like to thank some people who have given invaluable help and support in making this book possible—Dr. Gertrude Tharpe, WMU Editorial Department Director; Ann Kilner, Special Products editor; Pat Sullivan, the editor who began the project; Marti Solomon, Acteens consultant; Theresa Sapp, typist; Connie McNeill, proofreader and affirming critic; the many people who have offered insights and resources; and my special friends, who are teaching me the meaning of friendship.

Contents

Chapter 1
A Beginning

Rhonda, a high school junior, has been actively involved with her church youth group since the Sunday she was promoted into the youth department. In the past few months, she has wondered how she can better express her commitment to Jesus Christ when she is with friends at school. Her friends sense that she cares about them, and they admire her for the way she lives. Several of them have talked to her about problems they have. Sometimes Rhonda feels she does not know what to say or how to help.

Jan, a seventh-grader, is quiet and shy around people she does not know well. She has a few close friends, but she wishes she could get to know more people and talk more freely with other students. Jan is also trying to become more honest in sharing her feelings with her closest friends.

Eric, a ninth-grader, has a head full of questions about what it means to live as a Christian. He wonders how to know what is right or wrong in the many decisions he must make. He wants to share his faith in Christ with friends at church and school, but he has a hard time getting beyond surface conversations about classes, sports, and parties.

E ach of us can see something of ourselves in Rhonda, Jan, and Eric. Yet each of us is a unique individual. We are

Christians, and we want to know how to live our Christian faith more effectively on a day-to-day basis. Yet sometimes we question whether there is much we can do as we follow our daily routine of going to school, ball games, and rehearsals, talking to friends, and coming home.

One way in which we can begin to share our faith and meet the needs of people around us is by offering ourselves as friends. Being a friend means much more than saying hello, agonizing over a defeat by the football team, and eating lunch together in the cafeteria. It means listening when our friend is discouraged, helping that friend find solutions to problems, and continuing to show that we care.

Sometimes it is very difficult to be a friend. We are so excited about being elected to student government that we don't notice that a girl who lost is fighting back tears. The father of the boy who sits next to us in American history has a heart attack and dies, and we stare at our desks in embarrassment over not knowing what to say. Two girls laugh as they trade stories of how drunk they got Saturday night, and we laugh too, not wanting to appear different and lose their friendship.

This book is about a different kind of friend—one who gives freely to help others with their problems, questions, and disappointments. This is the kind of friend that Christ was talking about when he said, "The greatest love a person can have for his friends is to give his life for them" (John 15:13 TEV). This kind of friendship involves being willing to spend yourself for another person, to open your life to that person, and to share the best that you have. You take the risk of confidently standing by your friend in special times of need. You do not have to have all the answers, and sometimes you may say or do something that seems to hurt, rather than help. But you work at learning how to recognize needs, and you develop skills in meeting them. You start where you are, with the friends you have, and you begin to grow in your ability to help people.

The Bible will help us understand what it means to be a real friend. In Galatians 6:2 Paul writes, "Bear one another's burdens, and thus fulfill the law of Christ." We are not only to look out for our own interests and needs, but are consciously to grow sensitive to the needs of others (Phil. 2:4).

Our model in meeting the needs of others is Jesus Christ, who said, "A new commandment I give to you, that you love one another, even as I have loved you, that you also love one another" (John 13:34). The word Jesus used for love was *agape*, the creative, caring love which expresses the nature of God himself. This is the love that we received from God when we trusted Christ as Saviour. We respond to the love which Christ has shown us by expressing that same type of *agape* love to others. We read in the New Testament of Jesus reaching out in love to the blind, the crippled, the lonely, the searching, and the confused. As we read the Bible and pray, we can begin to see other people as Christ sees them. He will help us break through the masks of indifference, hate, or bitterness to see the real hurts which lie underneath and to respond to those hurts with his love.

Our faith is thus not only a matter of words, but also of actions that express love for friends when they need us (1 John 3:18). Often our caring deeds demonstrate the love of Jesus to friends who are not Christians and open the way for us to tell them about the difference Jesus can make in their lives. As we search for solutions to problems with a confidence in Christ's wisdom, we help our friends understand what it means to be a Christian.

Another way we can understand what it means to be a friend is by considering the persons we go to when we have a special need. What are they like? Why do we go to them?

We can probably name several distinctive characteristics of friends to whom we turn for help. **They are warm and loving.** We do not question whether they care because they show love through both words and actions. They enjoy being alone sometimes, but they are also eager to be around other people—to talk to them and to hear what they are thinking.

Our most helpful friends are constantly learning and growing. They know that it is almost impossible to help a friend go further in reaching solutions to problems than you have gone yourself.

Ted was playing forward in a tightly-contested basketball game between his school and their main rival for the district championship. The player guarding him was constantly jabbing an elbow into his ribs when the referee was not looking. Late in the game as the players shoved for position on a rebound, Ted was jabbed one time too many. He angrily pushed the guard away and, when 11 called for a foul, began complaining loudly about the rough play throughout the game. Ted's friend Bill leaped to his defense and furiously pointed out the cheap-shot play of the guard. After the game Ted felt ashamed and guilty about losing his temper, but Bill was too wrapped up in his own anger to help. He could not help Ted handle his feelings because he could not control his own temper. We must learn to deal with our own weaknesses in order to become effective in helping others with their problems.

We usually turn for help to someone who is willing to spend the time and energy our problem requires. A commitment to be someone's friend involves a willingness to give that person our full attention at the time of need. This is not always easy because people don't just have problems when it's convenient for us to

stop and help. Our friend may need us when we are cramming for a test, when we have been up late the night before, or when we are anxious to talk to someone else. Is it worth the effort to show we care in the middle of a busy day?

We share most openly with a person whose expressions of caring come across as honest and sincere. We trust a person whose actions and words carry the same message. One summer Jody met the daughter of a man who had just begun work in her father's office. As the two girls talked, Jody learned they would begin the same grade in junior high. She promised to introduce the new girl to her friends. The week before school started, one of Jody's friends planned a pizza party. Jody suggested that the new girl be invited. She asked her father if they could pick her up so that she would not arrive alone. Jody meant what she said when she offered to introduce the new girl to her friends; she proved it when she included her in a back-to-school pizza party.

Finally, if we would help others as our special friends have helped us, we must depend on the Holy Spirit to guide us in making friends, becoming sensitive to their needs, and knowing how to help. We do not have all the answers for ourselves or for our friends, but we can look to God to know where to begin to make a difference in our world.

We understand what it means to be a friend through our Bible study and through our observations of people who have been special friends to us.

Yet it is only through putting into practice what we read and observe that we are able to become effective as friends. We help our friends most when we take the risk of learning to reach out and care.

> *"This is My commandment, that*
> *you love one another, just as I*
> *have loved you."*
> *John 15:12*

13

Chapter 2

Some Basics

Rick's parents are getting a divorce, and he can't seem to cope with the situation. He has lost interest in church, sports, and even his friends. He's talking about quitting school.

Sharon is pregnant with her boyfriend's baby. She is afraid to tell her parents, but she knows she has to do something soon.

Lisa's mother is an alcoholic. Recently she has been drinking more, and life at their house is often almost unbearable. Lisa would like to leave, but she doesn't know what to do.

Jerry is experimenting with illegal drugs. He insists he's just having fun and that he'll stop before he gets into anything really dangerous. He seems unaware that the drugs are having bad effects on his personality.

Our friends have major problems like these as well as many day-to-day ups and downs. How do we help in such a wide variety of situations?

Whatever the situation, we can follow some basic guidelines:

Our relationship with a friend who is hurting may enable us to help when someone who is more skilled could not. Some adults 15 have studied for years to know how to help teenagers with problems. We may feel our friends would be better off if they talked over their problems with school counselors, a pastor, or a doctor—anyone who knows more than we do. Yet our friendship allows them to be less afraid to talk to us. They may share more freely because they believe we understand what they are feeling. They may be embarrassed to tell an adult about the problem, or they may not believe an adult can understand how a teenager feels. We may not know as much as a skilled adult about how to deal with the problem, but we may be of more help because our friend trusts us and listens to us.

A helping relationship is a two-way street. We help a friend with a problem, and that friend helps us. God does not expect us to be super friends, swooping down to solve one crisis before dashing off to rescue someone else from certain ruin, never pausing to seek rest or help for ourselves. Each of us has weaknesses. We must realize we are not perfect before we can offer much help to a struggling friend. We must never assume the role of a spiritual giant reaching down to help a lowly sinner. Rather we must reach out to offer help to friends in their need, knowing that we may soon need help ourselves.

Often we receive while we are giving. We may learn how to grieve and handle death as we reach out to a friend whose brother has just died. As we help a classmate understand why she cannot make friends, she may teach us to be more sensitive to lonely people who long to be included in our circle of friends. We may tutor a friend who is failing algebra, and he may rescue our science project from disaster.

Each person has different values, different ways of looking at life, and different ways of making decisions. We tend to expect everyone to react, think, and feel in exactly the same way we do. However, Jill may simply shrug her shoulders and go on when her boyfriend breaks up with her; Sally may begin thinking about committing suicide. Mark may have decided where he will go to college when he was in junior high; Bob may be agonizing over whether or not to go to college the summer after high school graduation. One way of reacting or deciding is not necessarily better than another; we are simply different people. The uniqueness

16

of each individual plays a big part in determining that person's needs. We must learn to meet our friends' needs, not the needs we expect them to have.

We need to discover the values we share with our friends. We can then build on these values in searching for solutions to problems. For example, Marsha had begun to smoke marijuana with some of her older friends in high school. Her friend Joyce was concerned. She felt Marsha should not become involved with using drugs in any way. As a Christian, Joyce believed she should keep her body a temple of God and not do anything that could be harmful to her health. Marsha was not a Christian, so Joyce's reasoning made no sense to her. However, Marsha regularly jogged, played tennis, and watched her weight. She and Joyce agreed on the value of good health. This shared value served as a starting point for Joyce to approach Marsha about the problem of marijuana.

We do not have to know all the answers to all problems. It is more important to become involved with our friends and to show them we care than it is to impress them with our brilliant insights. Most problems do not have easy answers. For instance, consider Lisa, whose mother is an alcoholic. There is no quick and easy solution that we can give Lisa. Whatever answers she and her family come up with will have to be struggled through and worked out over many months. We will only alienate Lisa if we shrug off the situation with sweet-sounding, glib advice. We can help her most by assuring her of the constancy of our friendship and by helping her discover the best methods for dealing with the situation.

A person must want to change or desire advice in order for us to help. Just as we cannot force a person to become a Christian, we cannot force a friend to seek help for excessive drinking or to resolve differences with a teacher. Sometimes people stubbornly refuse help because they are afraid that they cannot change or that there are no solutions to their problems. They may refuse our help because they do not yet trust us. We must help these friends have a sense of hope that change is possible and that they can trust us. Our natural tendency may be to become frustrated and give up. We may feel like failures. Our task is to maintain hope

17

and patiently prove ourselves trustworthy. If we can help our friends to believe they can change, they will have a much greater chance of doing so. This is true no matter how impossible change may seem and no matter how many mistakes we may make in trying to help.

It is important to accept our friends as they are and not demand that they change as a condition of our continuing friendship. When people are hurting or trying to handle a problem, their worst qualities often come out. They may be more angry, bitter, or hateful than usual, but they need a friend to accept them and care about them more than in the good times. Consider Jerry and his use of drugs. If we demand that he either stop using drugs immediately or lose our friendship, we will get nowhere. We will only encourage any suspicions he may have that we did not really care about him. Love must be a constant, not a reward that is offered if a hurting friend straightens out and meets our expectations.

We must constantly seek to broaden our circle of friends. We must learn to care about more than our closest friends at school, our Christian friends at church, or our family. We need to grow in our awareness of people we might enjoy knowing better. We can learn to look around us at people we know only slightly. They may need very much to know that we care about them. It is easy for us to pat ourselves on the back for the way we have helped our closest friends with their needs and not notice that we have ignored many other hurting people at the same time. We must be careful not to overlook people God may be leading us to help.

As we pray for God to show us the people he would have us help, he will make us aware of specific needs. We will find ourselves continually thinking about a person we can help. We will discover opportunities to begin a friendship or to meet a need of which we had not been aware.

Our ultimate aim in helping our friends is to lead them to know Jesus Christ who is the source of strength, wisdom, and love. We not only help them deal with an immediate problem, we also introduce them to Jesus Christ. He will help them deal with the greater problem of sin in their lives. We do not want our friends always to depend on us to handle each difficulty. We want them to grow more able to deal with problems through their relationship with Jesus Christ.

Just as we need to follow these basic guidelines in a helping relationship, we must also learn to avoid potential dangers.

Maintain a spiritual balance. If Rick comes to us to talk about his parents' divorce, he does not need to hear us quoting Scriptures about the home. He needs for us to listen carefully and to help him look for positive actions he can take in this situation. He needs to hear that we understand how hard it can be to put Christian principles into action. After all, many problems cannot be resolved with black-and-white answers; many answers must be grappled for in a vast gray area. We must be careful never to criticize a struggling friend for a lack of faith. This will destroy any chance we might have had to help him.

The flip side of this danger is a failure to witness to a friend, as well as to help with the immediate problem. When people are hurting or dealing with a serious problem, they may be most open to hearing about the love of Jesus Christ and accepting him as Saviour.

Avoid the temptation to be overly curious. We must be careful not to push our friends for more details about problems than they need to tell or feel comfortable giving. For example, if Sharon tells us that she is pregnant with her boyfriend's baby, we need to help her handle her guilt and make the necessary decisions about what she will do now. She may want help in knowing how to talk with her boyfriend and/or her parents. She does not need the pain of having to answer our questions about the details of their relationship.

Do not reveal what was told in confidence. The safest rule is "If in doubt, don't say it." We must be careful not to break any confidences as we explain a prayer request for a friend who has talked to us about a problem. For example, we may have good intentions when we ask our youth group to pray for Lisa's mother who is an alcoholic. However, Lisa may be humiliated that we have told this and never speak freely to us again.

Sometimes we break confidences by trying to impress other friends that a certain person has confided in us or that we have

19

discussed a serious problem with her. It is far better to say nothing than to risk breaking a confidence.

Treat a friend as a responsible person, not as a child. We must avoid the temptation to take over and solve our friends' problems for them. We may feel that we know the best thing for Sharon to do about her pregnancy, but we must not try to make her decision for her. If we do, we are saying, in effect, "I know you cannot handle this problem; let me do it for you." With this attitude we cause her to feel even more helpless and possibly to resent us.

Be a real friend, not a do-gooder. We are to be sensitive to people we can help, but we are not to run around straightening out everybody. The other person must desire our help, and we must give it in a nonjudgmental manner.

Avoid the dangers of sexual involvment with the person who needs help. We must be aware of our own sexual feelings, the feelings of the person we are helping, and the reactions of other people as they view our relationship. We may hug and touch a friend, and we may spend a great deal of time alone together as we talk over a problem. However, there is the possibility that our friend, boy or girl, may interpret our touching as a sign of sexual interest, rather than warm caring. If that friend touches us back in a way that makes us uncomfortable or indicates sexual interest, we need to explain that the relationship is one of friendship. Then we should refrain from further touching.

A danger sign in a friendship with a person of the same sex may be expressions of possessiveness or jealousy. Our friend's demands that we spend much of our time alone together do not necessarily indicate a homosexual leaning, but they do indicate an unhealthy turn in the relationship. We must firmly express our caring, but make it clear that we must also have other friends. The suspicions which an apparently exclusive friendship arouses in other people's minds may threaten our future opportunities to help people.

A girl, especially one who is physically attractive, must avoid placing herself in a situation where either she or a boy she is helping would face too much sexual temptation. If she has the slightest doubts, she should talk to the boy when other people are around. She must be especially cautious in helping a boy she does not know well. It would be foolish, for example, to meet a boy for the first time, begin talking to him about a problem, then get in a car alone with him. A boy who is helping a girl needs to take similar precautions to avoid unnecessary temptations. If we find the sexual side of a helping relationship getting out of control, we need to refer that person to someone else for help.

We will avoid many dangers of a helping relationship when we share out of what Jesus Christ has done for us, rather than out of our own need to be needed. The *agape* love that we received from Christ has as its goal the highest good of the recipient, and it seeks nothing in return. We have experienced this kind of love both directly from God and through other people. God has entrusted to us the special responsibility of sharing this love with people who need it.

A film entitled A *Desk for Billie*, produced by the National Education Association, tells the story of Billie Davis, the daughter of migrant workers who frequently moved from town to town. One day her elementary school teacher noticed Billie was having trouble seeing a book she was trying to read. The teacher made an appointment with a doctor for Billie to have her eyes checked, then paid for the glasses which he prescribed. When she gave the glasses to Billie one day after class, Billie said, "I can't take these; we've got no money." The teacher explained that she had once needed glasses as a little girl and could not afford them. Her teacher bought them for her and told her that someday she would buy glasses for another little girl and thus repay the debt. Billie's teacher said, "So you see, you can take the glasses; they were paid for a long time ago."[1]

We have been loved, and in response, we love others. We become a friend by putting into practice what we have seen of love and what we are learning daily.

> *"We love because God first*
> *loved us."*
> 1 John 4:19 (TEV)

[1]*Paul Welter*, How to Help a Friend (*Wheaton, Illinois: Tyndale House Publishers, Inc.*, 1978), p. 37.

Chapter 3
Making Friends

Barbara enjoyed high school a lot. She was active in a number of clubs and had several close friends who shared good and bad times with her. Then, just as she was beginning her junior year, her family moved to a new town. She didn't know ANYBODY. She wondered if she would ever have any friends as good as the ones she left behind.

Ralph spent a lot of time alone. He liked people, but he couldn't seem to find anything to talk to them about. It seemed that the guys all liked football, and the girls all liked guys who liked football. Ralph thought football was all right, but his real interest was music. He spent hours listening to opera recordings and he had a sizable collection. Ralph would have liked for someone to listen to these operas with him, but he was sure no one else in his school shared his interest. He wouldn't even bring it up for fear people would laugh.

Crystal was having trouble getting along with her parents. She and her father had a lot of arguments over dating, curfews, the car, and almost anything else that came up. Crystal had a hard time coping with this, but at least she had her friend Jenny to talk to. Every day as soon as she got to school Crystal found Jenny and gave her all the details of her latest problems at home. If she didn't finish before class started, she could always continue at lunch or after school. For 23 *a while Jenny was just great. She listened patiently and offered encouragement when she could. Then, after about a week, Jenny became harder to find. She was seldom at the place where Crystal usually met her before school, and when Crystal did find her, she was always in a hurry to go somewhere. Crystal began to get the hint—Jenny was tired of hearing about her problems. "Oh well," thought Crystal, "she wasn't a very good friend anyway. If she'd ever had problems of her own, she'd understand how I feel."*

What does it mean to be a friend? How does a friendship develop? Some of us seem to be constantly surrounded by people, while others of us have only a few friends. Yet all of us can learn how to move from the level of passing acquaintance to the level of friend in our relationships.

In order to meet people who might become our friends, we can become involved in organizations or go to events where we will find people with whom we have something in common. Through Acteens, RA, Sunday School, and other Christian organizations, we will meet persons who are likely to share our values. School organizations, such as Future Teachers of America, National Thespian Society, and American Field Service, appeal to students who share similar interests. If we enjoy sports, we can attend football and basketball games, join a pep club, or try out for a school or city-league sports team.

When our friends or organizations to which we belong sponsor parties or special events, we may meet new people or get to know acquaintances in a totally different way. A boy we assumed spent all his time in the chemistry laboratory may also turn out to be a terrific ping pong player. The girl we thought was such a snob may seem very friendly over a campfire on a backpacking trip. Going on overnight trips to conferences or camps may help us break out of our routines and get to know people better.

Running for student government or an office in a club can help us meet people. Then, if we are elected, we will learn how to work with people. When Barbara started to a new school as a junior, she decided to look for opportunities to meet people. She learned that in order to run for student government, she needed signatures from 25 people on a petition. Soon she had met 25 new people, had her name on the ballot, and was on her way to meeting many more during the election campaign.

A further step to making friends is simply to be ourselves. We will make more friends if we express our true feelings, interests, and opinions than if we try to say what we expect everyone else to say. Remember Ralph and his opera records? One day Ralph overheard Nancy telling some of her friends that she enjoyed opera. He excitedly found a chance to tell her about his record collection. Soon the two of them were getting together regularly to listen to music. A friendship developed because they discovered that they shared a unique interest.

When we meet persons who we feel might become our friends, we should not hesitate to ask them to do something or go someplace with us. We may want to tell them we like them and would like to know them better. People tend to respond in a friendly way when they learn someone likes them.

Above all, we must take the risk of the other person not returning our offer of friendship. We take risks in all stages of friendship. The other person may not like us, may do something to hurt us, or may move away and leave us feeling alone. Yet only through risk do we break through the surface, casual relationships to the deeper level of friendship.

As we become someone's friend, we must be willing to spend time together. When we begin taking our friends for granted, assuming they will be around when we want to do something or assuming they know what we are thinking, we begin to destroy our friendship. Friends need to feel wanted, and when we spend time with them, we show them that they are important to us.

Our friends also need to be accepted as they are, not molded into carbon copies of ourselves. Although we will find that we agree often and that we do many things in the same way, we may be surprised by some differences. Mary may talk constantly when she is nervous, while we become very quiet. At midnight Mike may be just getting started in having fun and talking; yet we may have been struggling since nine o'clock to keep our eyes open. We should learn to accept our differences and to appreciate our friends for their uniqueness as individuals. Perhaps we can learn why they do things in a different way.

We can go a step further and affirm our friends—help them feel like capable persons about whom we care deeply. We want them to feel as if they can relax and be themselves around us without 25

fear of being rejected. We affirm our friends by complimenting them, encouraging them, and asking them for help and advice.

At the same time that we tell our friends what we like about them, we must be very careful about criticizing them. Sometimes we may need to point out something they are doing that is harmful or that is offensive to other people. However, we must never take secret pleasure in pointing out faults "for their own good." A good check is that we should not say anything critical to a friend unless it hurts us to say it.

Another important aspect of friendship is listening to what our friends have to say. People like to feel that what they are saying is entertaining and worth attention. When we listen, we show that we are interested in who they are and what they are like. They will want to be around us when something exciting has happened or when they are struggling for a direction to go in handling a problem. They know they can count on us to listen. One of the greatest gifts we can give is our willingness to listen.

Sometimes two close friends may be so eager to tell each other what they have been doing that neither listens. Oddly enough, they might be better listeners if they were talking to complete strangers. We must be especially careful not to take our best friends for granted when we talk. We must listen as carefully as if we were just beginning a friendship.

We must carefully avoid the habit of expecting our friends to listen to our gripes, disappointments, and frustrations too much of the time. When we do this, we are treating our friends like garbage dumps—backing up and unloading all the ugly parts of our lives on them. Our friends also need to see us when we are cheerful. They need to hear us share the good things that are happening to us.

Remember Crystal and Jenny? Jenny was a good listener, and Crystal began to take advantage of her available ear. Crystal was not aware that she was becoming a burden to Jenny. She just thought that the sure way to keep Jenny's attention was to have a problem to talk about. Jenny wanted to be helpful, but she could not handle a constant menu of bad news. Sometimes she needed to talk about pleasant things like a funny incident in the biology lab or the football game that was coming up. Sometimes she needed someone to listen to her problems, for contrary to

Crystal's assumption, Jenny had problems too. She began avoiding Crystal, not because she didn't care about her, but because meaningful sharing has to be two-way, and it has to include the good as well as the bad.

Friendships are strengthened through the everyday thoughtful things two people can do for each other. When Jack is sick and misses several days of school, we can bring him class notes and homework assignments, or save him a copy of the school newspaper. If we know that Sally loves rocky road ice cream, we can treat her to an ice-cream cone when she is feeling low. Friends are appreciated when they take the time to think of small favors they can do to show someone they care.

Another key quality of friendship is the ability to allow our friends to have other friends and interests. We stifle our friends when we are jealous of the funny experiences or hobbies they share with other people. If we demand that they spend too much time with us, we will drive them away.

As we become closer to our friends, we will find ourselves revealing more of our inner thoughts. Our willingness to risk letting our friends see past our surface reactions will result in their feeling freer to share their hopes and fears with us. We will become better friends as we realize that we accept and enjoy each other for what we have hidden on the inside, as well as for what we make evident on the outside. When we reveal ourselves to another person, we find that we understand ourselves better. We make sense out of confusion when we speak our thoughts to a trusted friend. We learn how important values are to us when we express them to another.

Learning to share deeply with a friend is not something that happens overnight, but something that grows as we build our relationship. We should not reveal anything that would hurt our friend or another person. We need never reveal anything that we feel uncomfortable sharing. The time may or may not come when we share the most hurting or risky thoughts deep within us. We need feel no pressure to share before we can do so comfortably.

As we develop and put into practice the qualities of true friendship, we find ourselves making new and closer friends. Our ability to be a friend is not based on the number of our friends, but on the depth of our relationship with those friends we have. Being

28

popular is not the same thing as having friends. We will be good friends only as we find ourselves caring about each other and knowing we can count on each other.

> *"If God so loved us, we also ought to love one another."*
> 1 John 4:11

Chapter 4

Trust—
A Two-Way Street

Nancy frowned at her image in the mirror as she put the finishing touches on her makeup before her date with Greg. She remembered how she had once thought she would do almost anything to get him to look in her direction. When they were scheduled to take driver's education classes at the same time, she felt certain her opportunity had come.

The first day of class, Nancy waited in the hall until she saw Greg entering the classroom. She was proud of herself when she managed to appear very casual and to slide into a chair right beside his. Each day she had opportunities to talk to Greg for a few minutes before and after class. If he talked about a soccer match, she pretended to find it the most interesting sport of all. If he made fun of the girl on the front row in their class who was overweight, she laughed and was careful never to be seen talking to that girl again.

Finally, Greg asked Nancy to a movie. She was so excited that she must have tried on every blouse in her closet before deciding on the one he would like. After the movie was over, she waited to hear whether or not Greg liked it before she gave her opinion. On the way home, she looked up into the clear evening sky and thought how much she would like simply to look at the stars and imagine what pictures they seemed to form. Yet Nancy said nothing, afraid that Greg would think her thoughts were silly.

The movie date must have gone well, thought Nancy, because

Greg asked her out for another date, and then another. Yet tonight Nancy was feeling uneasy about going out with Greg again. She was so tired of always worrying about what he would think of everything she said or did. Greg was not dating the real Nancy; he only knew the Nancy she pretended to be. Tonight she was going to tell him that she had been hiding her honest thoughts and feelings.

Maybe Greg would bring her back home immediately when he found out what she was really like. She imagined the embarrassment she would feel when her friends called to ask what had gone wrong.

On the other hand, maybe Greg would like her better when he knew her honest reactions. He might be growing tired of dating a girl who would only parrot his opinons. Maybe Greg even enjoyed looking at the stars and imagining the pictures they were forming.

Nancy breathed a deep sigh as the doorbell rang. "Well, I might be seeing you again real soon," she said to the stuffed cat on her bed as she flipped out the light.

Nancy took the risk of being open with Greg—of letting him know her as she really was. The thud-thud of her heart and the shaky feeling in her stomach told her how afraid she was of taking the risk of being honest.

Many of us fear that others will not like us, will no longer want to be our friends, or, worst of all, will make fun of us if they know us as we are. We sometimes think that the more we tell them about ourselves, the more they will back away from us. However, just the opposite is often true. The more we disclose of ourselves, the more likely our friends are to want to be around us. This turned out to be the case with Nancy and Greg. When she began letting him see the real Nancy, their relationship grew. Of course, they agreed on some things and disagreed on others, but they began to trust each other to express their real feelings. As a matter of fact, Greg confessed to Nancy that although he had enjoyed their dates in the past, he had wondered what she was really like. He had wanted to move beyond surface politeness in their conversations, but he had not known how—as long as Nancy revealed so little about herself. Now they could work together to build an honest relationship.

Being open about our feelings does not mean always talking about ourselves or insisting on giving our opinion on every subject. It does not mean digging into all the dark corners of our mind to reveal the most personal details of our past. Being open means honestly expressing how we feel at the present moment.

In a growing, healthy friendship, we learn to discuss things that upset or disturb us. If we try to ignore our feelings or push upsetting incidents to the back of our minds, we are likely to explode in anger later. We may try to convince ourselves that a hurtful comment by a friend does not bother us. However, we find that comment creeping up again and again in our minds. The more we think about it, the worse it may sound to us. We may start to remember other times that friend has hurt us, or we may imagine hateful comments our friend could say in the future. The one hateful comment looms larger and larger as we try to push it out of our thoughts. If we bring our honest feelings out in the open, we can relieve the tension with our friend. We can thus prevent the comment from driving a widening wedge into our relationship.

When we have been hurt or wronged and have decided to be open with our friends, we must talk about our own feelings regard-

ing the situation. We must not begin by accusing our friends or guessing what they might have been thinking when they did something that hurt us. For example, we could say, "It hurts me when you interrupt in the middle of my telling a story and finish it yourself," not "You're so rude."

We should also avoid calling our friends names out of anger, jealousy, or a desire to point out their faults, as in "You were so cocky when Mrs. Thomas selected you to read your English essay in the school assembly." When we begin comments to our friends with phrases such as "you never" or "you always," we are making unfair judgments about them. We also need to watch our conversations to see that we are not ordering our friends around, being sarcastic, or accusing them of negative motives for their actions. ("You just invited Jeff to our youth group so he could vote for you to be president.") Being open and honest does not mean making unkind remarks to others. When we take the risk of being honest about our feelings, other people may discover our faults. However, we do not use our honesty as an excuse for pointing out the faults of others.

We have to use good judgment in opening ourselves to friends. When we are first getting to know each other, we will naturally be less open. As our friendship develops, we will share on a deeper level. Generally, we begin talking to people about things, then move to ideas, and finally discuss our feelings when we are closer friends.

Dave and Larry became friends when they worked together in the grocery store. They found they enjoyed discussing their favorite automobiles and the weekend's football scores. As they got to know each other better, they talked about ideas: whether it was more important to buy a car now or to save money for college and what they were looking for in a college. Later they began to share their feelings: Larry was afraid his father would take a job in another town before his senior year in high school. Dave was afraid his grades weren't good enough for a college scholarship, and he knew his parents couldn't pay his college expenses.

The time may come when we are open with our friends and they take advantage of us or break a confidence. Suppose Larry started rumors that Dave probably wasn't going to get into college because his grades weren't good enough and he didn't have the money. Dave would be sorry he had trusted Larry, and he might even feel that he could never trust anyone else again.

What can we do when our friends betray our trust like this? Without accusing or judging, we can tell them how hurt or angry we feel about their breaking a confidence. They may or may not apologize, but we must still forgive. Forgiveness does not mean that we forget their actions and continue to talk with them on the same trust level. We have learned that we must be very careful about what we say to them because they may use our words to hurt us. Although we may not share deeply with those persons, we still can show ourselves friendly and forgiving through a smile, a willingness to converse, and other acts of caring. They may learn about forgiveness from us, and one day they may turn to us in need of a friend.

Discovering that one friend cannot be trusted should not cause us to lose faith in all of our friends. We may need to tell our other friends that we are afraid to trust them because we have been hurt. They may help by allowing us to pour out our hurt and sorrow to them. We are sometimes hurt through the risk of friendship, but to build a wall around our feelings is to guarantee loneliness.

Building a climate of trust not only involves being open with our friends. We must also allow them to be open with us. Nancy made an important decision when she took the risk of being open with Greg. It is just as important for her to look for opportunities to encourage Greg to be open with her. The road to trust must be paved in both directions. We encourage our friends to be open when we accept them as persons, even if we disagree with their words or actions. One way we can show our acceptance is by listening to them in a sincere attempt to understand their point of view. When we take their words seriously, they are more likely to feel they can trust us and share their feelings openly. They can let their guard down when they know they do not have to argue and defend their every word. We may not agree with their opinion. However, we can respect them enough to listen closely in order to understand the reasons for their feelings.

When our friends are open with us, we must be careful not to laugh, ridicule, crack a joke, or make light of what they have shared. We may nervously want to lighten the conversation by saying something funny, but a friend sharing a serious thought or feeling may not appreciate or understand our humor. 35

We should also avoid moralizing or passing judgment through statements such as "I told you so" or "That's what happens when you run around with someone like that." If our friends are feeling guilty over something they have said or done, they do not need us to heap more guilt on them or tell them that what they did was all right. They need our acceptance and support as they make amends or otherwise cope with their wrong actions.

In helping our friends to be open, we need to avoid using the phrase, "I know how you feel." We can seek to understand our friends' feelings, but we are different people and cannot completely understand, even if we have had a similar experience. To say we know how they feel tends to cut off the conversation and take away their freedom to keep talking. We also should avoid other trite phrases, such as "Is there anything I can do?" and "You must feel terrible."

Our friends will feel the freedom to be open when we answer their disclosures by affirming them. If we are silent, our friends may wonder if we are rejecting them because of what they have told us or if we simply do not care. They may be afraid that they have revealed too much. On the other hand, if we respond by accepting our friends and assuring them that we care, they will feel free to continue their openness with us.

We also help our friends to trust us when we go out of our way to show them that we care. When we do this, we lessen their risk in being honest with us. As we strengthen the climate of trust in our relationship, we find that we are more able to help each other with special needs.

> "Let us not love with words
> or tongue but with actions and
> in truth."
> 1 John 3:18 (NIV)

Chapter 5

Getting Through to a Friend

Two dejected men walked toward Emmaus one afternoon, sadly recounting the events of the past few days in Jerusalem. A stranger appeared beside them and asked what they were discussing that troubled them so. One of the men, Cleopas, replied, "Are you the only one visiting Jerusalem and unaware of the things which have happened here in these days?" The men poured out their sorrow and confusion at the Crucifixion of Jesus Christ, then the amazing discovery three days later that his body was not in the tomb where he had been laid.

After listening carefully to the two men, the stranger began to explain the Scriptures that showed how the recent events in Jerusalem were part of God's plan. The three men reached Emmaus in the evening and sat down to eat supper. As the stranger blessed and broke the bread, the two men recognized their companion as Jesus Christ himself. After he disappeared from sight, they said, "Were not our hearts burning within us while he was speaking to us on the road, while he was explaining the Scriptures to us?" They immediately got up from the supper table and returned to Jerusalem to assure the disciples that Jesus had indeed risen from the dead.[1]

Jesus helped the two men handle their grief over what they thought had happened to him. He began by listening, asking a question that allowed them to pour out all their hurt and disappointment. When they had finished talking, they were able to listen to Jesus and finally to see who he really was.

We too can help our friends by learning how to listen. We can put into practice the advice of James 1:19: "Let every one be quick to hear, slow to speak and slow to anger." If we are always talking, we cannot understand or respond to the needs of our friends. Our listening shows them that we care.

When someone is talking to us, we show that we are listening by establishing eye contact. At first we might feel uncomfortable looking at our friends' eyes as they talk. Eye contact will seem more natural as we carefully concentrate on what they are saying. We will also find ourselves leaning forward as we pay close attention to their words.

We need to listen to our friends' words, rather than thinking about how we will answer or what we will say next. Sometimes we begin to panic inside because we are afraid we have nothing helpful to say. The more we worry about what we will say, the less we are able to listen. We are better off relaxing. When we have no answer, we can say, "I'm feeling very much with you right now, but I simply do not know what to say," or "I think I understand what you mean, but I can't think of any helpful answer to make right now."[2]

Sometimes a friend is talking to us, and we discover that we are thinking about ourselves and a problem of our own. When we cannot get a problem out of our minds, we know we need to seek help. We are unable to help others when we can think only of our own problems.

We should be careful not to interrupt our friends when they are talking to us. If someone else interrupts us, such as when the phone rings and no one else is around to answer it, we need to remember what our friend is saying and return the conversation to that point when the interruption is over. We can help our friend begin talking again by starting "You were saying . . ."

As we listen, we need to be careful that we do not assume that we already know everything our friend is going to say. We may grow impatient if we already know the facts of an incident our friend is relating. However, we can listen even more carefully to know how our friend views the incident. Sometimes we even need to listen patiently to the same story told a second or third time by the same person.

40

We also need to be sure that we do not consider talking to be more important than listening. Sometimes our friends will work out their own solutions by simply explaining a problem to us. They may need someone to listen to their hurt and respond by loving them, not by coming up with an answer.

Jack had tried out for the lead in the school drama. When the cast list was posted, his name was listed by a very minor part. Mark found him all alone on the racquetball court, and he could tell he

was upset by the way he was slamming the ball. Mark ventured, "I heard about the cast list, and I know how much you wanted that big part."

"Yeah, well, who cares?" Jack retorted as he gave the ball an extra hard slam. Then he lashed out in anger at the drama teacher and the students who had the lead parts. "I haven't got time for drama anyway. I've got better things to do. They can find somebody else for the minor characters."

Mark didn't know what to say, so he didn't say anything at all. That was just as well really. Jack didn't need someone to defend the drama teacher, or to assure him that he really deserved the part. He simply needed someone to listen.

We can protect our friends by being careful that they do not tell us something in a moment of stress that they will later regret. If we suspect they will be sorry they have told us so much, we can stop them and ask if they are certain they feel comfortable with our knowing these things. For instance, if Jack began telling Mark harmful information about the student who got the part he had tried out for, Mark could find a way to ask him not to discuss that person while he was so upset. This would save Jack from the embarrassment of having said the wrong thing in a weak moment.

Another part of being a good listener is learning how to respond to what our friends are saying. We can ask leading questions that will help them understand the way they feel. Some possible leading questions are:[3]

What worries you the most about _____?
If you had your choice, what would you do?
How do you feel about it?
To get this done, what will you need to do?
And if that fails, what will you do?
Can you remember how it happened?
Can you describe it in your own words?
Are there any other angles you can think of?

Through such questions, we can help to put our friends in touch with their emotions. We can help them identify their feelings by asking a question such as, Did you feel angry when that happened? Sometimes they will not understand or will try to avoid

42

facing their feelings. When that happens, we can suggest how they must be feeling. They can then either agree with us or explain that their feelings are quite different from what we think.

Mary might say, "It's that stupid teacher's fault that I failed the test. If he had explained how to do our math homework better, I could have worked the problems."

We might answer, "You sound really frustrated and angry over failing that test."

Mary might respond, "That's exactly how I feel," then go on to talk more about the test. By listening and asking leading questions, we could help her decide what to do next about her math grade. It would be more helpful to begin by talking to Mary about how she feels rather than recounting the exact facts of the situation.

Our friends seldom come to us asking for advice. They usually want us to listen to them, then help them make their own decisions. We must carefully avoid trying to talk them into doing what we think they should do. They may later resent us if they feel we pushed them into a course of action.

However, our friends will sometimes ask for our opinion or advice. When that happens, we need to give an honest answer without hedging. Gary was considering accepting an offer of a part-time job at a restaurant, but he had been told he would have to work every other Sunday. He asked a friend he respected what she thought about his working on Sundays. He wanted to hear what she honestly thought. As part of deciding what to do, he was asking for a friend's valued opinon.

When our friends talk to us about a problem, we may sometimes repeat in our own words what they have said. We can then be more sure that we understand what they mean. At other times they may be so upset that they are not thinking clearly. We may help them understand what they are trying to say by making a statement beginning, "What I hear you saying is . . ." or "What I think you mean is . . ."

When we respond to a friend, we should speak warmly, honestly, and calmly. If we feel ourselves catching our friend's panic or stress, we can consciously slow our voices down. We are then better able to remain calm and to calm our friend. We should speak confidently and firmly. The strength of our confidence will help our friend handle the problem.

We need to match as closely as possible the depth of our friend's comments or move to a slightly deeper level. In other words, if our friend is speaking seriously, we should respond seriously. If he is speaking on a shallow level, our responses cannot be very intense or deep.

Our responses to our friends should be brief, generally no more than one or two sentences in length. This keeps the focus on our friend who is talking, and it keeps the conversation rolling. Jesus' conversation with the Samaritan woman, recorded in John 4, can serve as a model for short responses. Each time Jesus spoke, he responded briefly and directly to the Samaritan woman. He did not offer a long speech or sermon, but he helped her through the give-and-take of conversation.[4]

When our friends have sinned, they may need us to listen to their confessions and then pray for them. In James 5:16, we read, "Confess your sins to one another, and pray for one another." We should not be shocked or condemn our friends' wrong actions; neither should we accept these actions. We can hear our friends' confessions. Then we can support them as they seek with God's help to change their actions.

As we respond to friends who are not Christians, we will need to be careful not to use churchy language. Our friends may not understand words like *salvation, grace,* and *redemption.* They may feel those words are the language of a clique to which they do not belong. We can communicate the same ideas in simpler, clearer terms. To do this, we must be sure we understand these terms ourselves. We may want to ask a more mature Christian to help us with these terms.

The purpose of our response to our friends is not to find out more about their actions and feelings to satisfy our own curiosity. Rather we want to help them understand their problems more clearly. Then they can take appropriate actions to make a change.

Communication takes many forms. We constantly communicate through our tone of voice, eye contact, posture, gestures, and facial expressions. All these factors combine to influence the total message that we convey.

44

Margie saw her friend Peg come rushing down the hallway at

school. She was smiling broadly, and her eyes were open wide with just a hint of a tear in the corners. Her hands were shaking slightly as she grasped Margie's arm. She leaned close, and the words seemed to tumble out of her mouth. Margie knew something wonderfully exciting had happened before Peg said anything. Sure enough, Peg had just learned she had been chosen to represent their school at a state convention for outstanding students.

We learn to read our friends' feelings by observing the way they look, dress, and speak. Some of their nonverbal communication can be seen in the following chart:[5]

Nonverbal Cue	Warmth	Coldness
Tone of voice	Soft	Hard
Facial expression	Smiling, interested	Frowning, disinterested
Posture	Lean toward other, relaxed	Lean away from other, tense
Eye contact	Look into other's eyes	Avoid looking into other's eyes
Touching	Touch other gently	Avoid touching other
Gestures	Open, welcoming	Closed, guarding oneself and keeping others away
Distance from People	Close	Distant

There are many varieties of meaning in nonverbal communication. Some people express fear by backing away. If John is part of a group and he does not agree with the group's decision, he may back his chair slightly out of the circle. Susan communicates caring by putting an arm around a friend's shoulder. Margaret cares just as deeply but she may only commuicate it through her facial expression and eye contact. When Mike clenches his fist, he is usually angry. Jim may clench his fist from fear or anxiety. Similar anxiety may cause Sandra to restlessly pull her hair. Nancy may wear loud or unusual clothes because she needs to call attention to herself. Paul's sloppy, unkempt appearance may be a sign of rebellion or dissatisfaction with himself.

We need to observe carefully our friends' expressions and gestures, but we must not jump to a quick conclusion based on nonverbal cues. Beth may be crying because she is very happy or because she is very sad. Her silence may mean that she doesn't care or that she is thinking deeply. She may slouch both when she is physically tired and when she has been greatly disappointed.

Just as we are aware of what other people are telling us through nonverbal communication, we need to be aware of the signals we are sending to them. We can work at giving out warm nonverbal cues. By smiling, we are communicating warmth and openness to others, and we are saying, "I like you." We can practice looking into others' eyes and speaking softly, but firmly.

Touching can be our best way of showing our friends who are hurting that we care. We might hug them, put our arm around their shoulders, or put our hand over theirs—whatever touching gesture both of us feel comfortable with. A touch of warmth can calm persons who are upset and bring them into better touch with present reality. If they are crying out of loneliness or grief, they may simply need to know that we are there. When we touch them, we tell them that we are with them, both physically and emotionally.

At times we may help friends understand the nonverbal cues they are sending out. They may need to know that their harsh, loud voices repel people. If they are upset and mumbling or talking too rapidly, we may gently encourage them to speak more clearly. This may enable them to get a better handle on their problems.

Listening, responding, and communicating nonverbally are valuable skills which take much work. We become stronger and better friends as we practice these important forms of communication.

> *"Words from the mouth of a*
> *wise man are gracious."*
> *Ecclesiastes 10:12*

[1]*Luke 24:13-35.*
[2]*Paul Welter*, How to Help a Friend *(Wheaton, Illinois: Tyndale House Publishers, Inc., 1978), p. 202.*
[3]*Mimi and Don Samuels*, The Complete Handbook of Peer Counseling *(Miami: Fiesta Publishing Corp., 1975), pp. 100-102.*
[4]*Welter*, How to Help a Friend, *pp. 205-209.*
[5]*David W. Johnson*, Reaching Out *(Englewood Cliffs, New Jersey: Prentice-Hall, Inc., 1972), p. 109.*

Chapter 6

Ways of Helping

Lynn's brother Ted was seriously injured in a car accident. There is doubt about whether he will ever walk again. Lynn is trying to be supportive of Ted and the rest of the family in this trying situation, but sometimes the stress at home is more than she can take.

Bob has been a Christian for three years. He is growing in his faith through personal study and participation in the church youth group. Bob is very concerned about his father, who doesn't attend church. He says Christianity just doesn't make sense to him. Bob wants to witness to his father, but he has a hard time doing so.

Bill needs to talk to his parents about the cost of college. His father has always believed Bill would get a football scholarship, but Bill knows this is not very likely. He is afraid to bring up the subject because he doesn't want to disappoint his father.

Carla wants to lose weight, but the situation seems hopeless. She has set a goal of losing 20 pounds, but she is afraid she will never reach it. Every time she tries to diet, she loses one or two pounds and then gets discouraged.

Judy has come home drunk several nights. This has hurt her parents and caused them to lose some of their trust in her. Judy has *realized that getting drunk is only hurting her, and she is determined to stop drinking. She is ashamed of disappointing her parents, and she wants them to trust her again.*

Our friends experience a wide variety of stressful situations. They may vary just as widely in the ways they react to their problems. One may retreat to her room and want to be left alone; another may want to be surrounded by friends. One may dig into his homework and study harder than ever; another may quit studying altogether. One will suddenly grow quiet and serious; another talks loudly and acts silly. Each person has a unique way of reacting to problems and escaping stress. Each may need a unique kind of help from us.

As we get to know our friends, we will observe the ways they react when they are facing problems. Some people get sick when they are upset or anxious about a situation. They do not get sick on purpose, but their illness may help them delay facing the problem or gain them sympathy from others. Other people find an outlet in sleep. They feel too tired to handle their stress at the moment, so they sleep and escape from it.

Escaping our problems is not necessarily bad. Sometimes we can step away and gain strength to deal with them later. Lynn, whose brother was seriously injured, needs to get away from the stress occasionally. A strenuous game of tennis may provide relief from her worries, and it may help her return to her family better able to help. This kind of escape will also enable her to keep a better hold on her own emotions. The only danger lies in the possibility that Lynn would spend so much time playing tennis that she would refuse to face her concern about her brother and her family's need for help. In that case, a healthy means of escape would turn into a barrier to dealing with reality.

Sometimes our friends experience stressful situations that are too much for them to handle, and they need our help. We have a unique privilege if we are there when they need us. "For if either of them falls, the one will lift up his companion. But woe to the one who falls when there is not another to lift him up" (Eccl. 4:10).

There are many ways we can help our friends find relief from stress. We can begin by being sensitive enough to their reactions to know when something is worrying them even if they have not said anything. We can do little things like writing notes and leaving them in their lockers or some other place they will be sure to find them. We can write a few words of encouragement or draw a cartoon. If we see a cartoon in the newspaper that a friend would enjoy, we can cut it out and enclose it in a note.

We can also send cards on birthdays, special days, or just any day that needs brightening. We can search for cards that contain exactly the right message—cards that our friends will know were carefully picked just for them. We can also make our own cards. Martha's cards were especially valued by her friends because they knew she had taken the time to draw a picture, pick out a photograph or quotation, or compose a poem just for them.

Sometimes our friends need help that requires more commitment from us than sending cards and notes. A friend whose home life is constantly unpleasant may need to experience a family setting in which members relate lovingly to each other. We can invite that friend to have supper, go on a picnic, or play board games with our family.

Sometimes the best thing we can do is to realize that someone else can help better than we can. Remember Bob who wanted to witness to his father? Jim tried to help Bob, but he realized that since he had grown up in a Christian home, he couldn't really identify with Bob's situation. However, Jim also knew Fred who was just beginning to experience some success in witnessing to his own father. Jim introduced Bob to Fred. Now Bob and Fred share their ideas, and Fred has helped Bob not to give up on his father. Jim was wise enough to know that a person dealing with a problem can often be helped by talking with someone who is facing or has faced a similar situation. This is a valuable experience if the two friends help each other deal positively with their situations rather than just feeling sorry for each other. We perform a valuable service to our friends when we introduce them to persons who have had problems similar to theirs.

Many people who are facing problems find help through participation in group or individual recreational activities. Swimming may help to get rid of tension. Being on the volleyball or track team can provide a feeling of belonging. Participation in clubs and other groups, such as the newspaper staff, the band, or the play

51

crew, can add a sense of purpose to life. If our friends are depressed or discouraged by their problems, they may need our encouragement to get involved in these activities.

Learning new skills may help take our friends' minds off their troubles and give them greater confidence. They may feel they have failed in one aspect of their lives, but they can experience success in another area. They may learn to play racquetball, to rollerskate, or to cook Chinese food. Crafts can be especially helpful for persons who worry a great deal about the future or who constantly live in a dream world. They will be forced to concentrate on the present moment as they sew a cross-stitch pattern or paint a ceramic plaque.

Reading books, watching television, or going to movies helps some people. They find escape from their problems for a little while, and they may find possible solutions. If we give a friend a book or invite her to a movie, we may discover an easy beginning point to discuss her situation.

We can help our friends increase their sense of personal worth through encouraging them to develop their unique talents and abilities. If they enjoy drama or music, they may be helped by performing and gaining applause for their skills. Persons interested in painting, sculpture, or photography may receive praise for their artwork and pictures. This praise may sustain them through hard times at home or broken relationships.

If they enjoy writing, they may keep a diary or journal in which they pour out their feelings. One of the main advantages of a journal is that they can go back and read it weeks or months later and see how they have progressed in dealing with their problems. They may also find help in writing letters to friends. We often understand our thoughts more clearly when we write them down.

People who enjoy nature may find release as they hike through the woods or along the beach, explore a new passageway in a cave, or sit on a riverbank fishing for perch. They may find their tensions easing as they get away from the phone, television, and other distractions and simply gaze at the beauty of God's world. They may begin to think more clearly and realize what values, people, and activities are most important.

Going to school activities and spending time with friends sometimes help. Sometimes people need to make new friends. They
may get to know new people in their school or neighborhood.

They may go to a summer camp or conference to meet people from other towns.

Getting a job may help our friends. It will allow them to be away from home for a while, and it will give them a sense of independence. A job will also bring them into contact with another group to which they can belong. The extra money may help with problems related to finances.

Friends with questions about God will find help through involvement in church youth activities. We can help them know how to begin a daily devotion time or work out a plan to memorize Scripture. Through Bible study we will be able to share our Christian convictions and explore what God has to say about different aspects of our lives. As we witness to non-Christians or search for answers to questions about the Bible, we may want to ask someone else, such as our pastor, Acteens leader, or youth director, to help us. We do not need to feel that we must have all the answers, and we should be careful not to offer pat or easy answers to our friends' questions.

When we talk to our friends about moral standards, we should have an attitude of humility. None of us are above temptations. We can help our friends come to conclusions about moral questions without setting ourselves up as the standard of perfection. We must avoid using Scriptures to prove our point, but we should allow the Holy Spirit to speak through them. The difference is one of attitude—either we rely on our own persuasiveness and ability to quote Scripture, or we trust God to speak through us and the Bible.

Often we can help our friends by offering encouragement. People may react differently to the same words. We must watch individual reactions to learn how each person is encouraged. Encouragement is not pushing our friends to do what we think they should do or falsely reassuring them that everything will turn out all right in the end.

Look back to the paragraph about Bill at the beginning of this chapter. He is afraid to talk to his parents. Suppose he comes to us for help. If we are being pushy, we might say, "Of course you should talk to them. Why don't you just do it tonight and get it over with?" If we are being falsely reassuring, our reply might be: 54 "I'm sure that if you talk to them, they'll understand perfectly.

You have nothing to worry about." An encouraging answer could be: "I can see you having the courage to sit down and talk with your parents just as you did with me. I know it won't be easy for you or them, but I believe you can do it."

Some friends may be encouraged by our pointing out the things they do well; others might feel we are only saying good things to make them feel better. Some friends may be reassured as we point out their courage in dealing with a situation; others might be frightened into inaction. As we observe our friends closely, we will begin to know what words will be most encouraging to them.[1]

We may have a friend who feels overcome by everything he has to get done. We can help him look at the choices before him, rather than the impossibility of getting the whole mass of work done. He can make a list of all he must do and set up a timetable for completing the tasks. He may have to decide which activities are most important and which ones can be eliminated. He may choose the jobs to which he will give most of his energy and those he will simply complete without trying to do them perfectly. We can help him concentrate on doing one thing at a time. Trying to accomplish everything at once only leads to frustration.

We can also help a friend who is working toward a goal that seems impossible to reach. Remember Carla who wanted to lose 20 pounds? Her friend Fran helped her find a good diet and exer-

cise plan. She helped her set up a series of smaller goals on the way to the magic 20 pounds. She agreed to go shopping with Carla as a reward for losing the weight. Most important, Fran remembered to give Carla regular encouragement along the way.

Sometimes a friend who has done something which harmed someone else may want to make amends, and she may need our help to know what to do. Consider Judy who had been coming in drunk. Now that she has decided to assume responsibility for her actions, we can suggest ways she can regain her parents' trust. She might voluntarily set a curfew for herself and take more responsibility with the housework.

We may help some friends by making task agreements with them. They may decide to deal with some negative side of their personalities by deciding upon something they will do daily to improve. We may also choose something we will do daily to improve ourselves. Then we can check on each other to see how we are doing and to encourage each other.

Susan was very withdrawn and shy. She decided she would do two things each day: consciously smile at one person and begin a conversation with someone.[2] Her friend Terry felt he had been too critical of people. He chose to compliment one person daily. They helped each other by checking on their progress each day.

People need help from us in many different ways. As we get to know them and reach out to them, we will find new ways to help. Sometimes we will make mistakes and do or say something that doesn't help at all. We keep trying and learning and giving. Our friends will likely appreciate us for our attempts to help and show we care, even when we do something wrong. We learn that a real friend is not something we become overnight; it is a goal toward which we grow.

> *"Oil and perfume make the*
> *heart glad, So a man's counsel is*
> *sweet to his friend."*
> Proverbs 27:9

[1]*Paul Welter,* How to Help a Friend *(Wheaton, Illinois: Tyndale House Publishers, Inc., 1978), pp. 146-7.*
[2]*Ibid., p. 181.*

Chapter 7

When We Can't Agree

Steve failed three out of five courses in the first quarter of school. Discouraged and worried, he turned to his friend Susan for help. Susan listened calmly as Steve went through the reasons for failing each class. Together they began to work out a plan for Steve to pass. He decided how much time he needed to study each day and what activities he needed to cut back in order to have plenty of time for studying.

One month later Steve was back to his old habits. Often he didn't take any books home, and he looked for excuses to go out with friends when he needed to study. Soon he was complaining to Susan again about his grades. She had already listened carefully and had helped him plan how to raise his grades. Now she knew she must confront him with the results of his actions. He said he wanted to pass, but he didn't act as if he did. Susan was afraid Steve would become angry or refuse to listen, but she knew she had to point out the inconsistency of his behavior.

Sometimes we can listen, help our friends come up with possible solutions to problems, and offer encouragement, but still they will not deal with the situation. The time has come to confront them—to lead them firmly, but gently, to face up to their actions.

We may sometimes need to confront our friends with sin in 59 their lives. For example, Joan's friend Brenda had been cheating on her Spanish tests. Joan had tried to overlook her suspicions that she was copying the work of the person seated next to her, but she finally had to admit that her suspicions were true. She had to confront her friend about what she was doing.

At other times we will need to confront our friends about the inconsistencies between their words and actions. ("You say you want to be a better friend to Mike, but you almost never talk to him.") Our friends may also have a tendency to evade issues. ("You claim to want to improve your appearance, but almost everytime anyone says something to help you, you change the subject.") A friend who is involved with a harmful habit or activity will also need to be confronted. ("I become concerned when I see you taking more and more tranquilizers all the time.")[1]

We often hesitate actually to confront our friends. We may be afraid they will reject us and never listen to us again. They might make fun of us, or they might lash back in anger. However, the most caring response and the greatest act of friendship may be to lead our friends to face up to the harm or destructiveness of their actions.

When we confront our friends about their problems, we must have inwardly committed ourselves to greater involvemenet with them. We must be willing to help them deal with their harmful actions. A confrontation is actually a request for a friend to make a change in actions or attitudes. Such changes will require our help and support.

The strength and quality of our relationship with a friend will determine how much we are able to say in a confrontation. Generally, the stronger the friendship, the stronger the confrontation. We do not have a responsibility to tell everyone in our school about their wrong actions; the freedom to confront is a right earned in the process of friendship.

It is important to consider the timing of our confrontation. Friends who are feeling especially down on themselves or who are very worried about something may not be able to act on our suggestion that they change some part of their lives. We need to wait for another time to confront them.[2]

Our attitude in confrontation is of utmost importance. The purpose of our words should be to help and heal, not to condemn or judge. Our friends may feel threatened or insecure when we point out harmful habits in their lives. They need to feel our support and affirmation. We might even say, "We will still be friends; it's just that I'm concerned about this part of your life."

We must be careful that we do not play God and set ourselves up as a perfect model. In Galatians 6:1, we read, "Even if a man is caught in any trespass, you who are spiritual, restore such a one in a spirit of gentleness, looking to yourselves, lest you too be tempted." Our attitude combines toughness and tenderness— toughness in facing the hard reality of sin and tenderness in encouraging our friends as they seek to change. Even as we confront our friends, we should examine our own lives for flaws and weaknesses. We may not take drugs, but we may sin by adopting a smug, superior attitude toward those who do.

Several types of confrontation are possible. The most basic type is to tell our friends how we see their actions and their consequences and how we react to what they are doing. Another possibility is to tell our friends what we believe their actions could lead to or why their actions or attitudes are harmful. In this case we offer opinions based on facts, instead of facts alone. Before speaking, we should try to understand the other person's feelings as fully as possible. An ancient Indian prayer tells us, "Grant that I may not criticize my neighbor until I have walked a mile in his moccasins." Our confrontation should be brief and not sound like an accusation. To be helpful, our words must help our friends know that we genuinely care about them.[3]

We may become angry in the middle of a confrontation. It is all right to express anger as along as we follow immediately with an expression of warmth. We should avoid expressing anger around other people. If we cause our friend to lose face in front of them, we may lose any future opportunity to help.

When friends are able to express anger to each other and see that the friendship survives, the quality of that friendship will actually grow stronger. The freedom to express differences and confront harmful actions in each other can lead to tighter bonds of caring.

A basic rule for confrontations is that we should help a person concentrate on her strengths and abilities, rather than her weaknesses and failures. Sarah had been helping her friend Barbie during a period when her parents were getting a divorce and her brother ran away from home. Barbie often visited in Sarah's home and had long talks with both Sarah and her mother. She felt accepted and loved in the middle of a hard time in her own home. Yet Barbie began to depend on Sarah too much. She went to her house every day, changed her class schedule to match Sarah's, and waited for her by her locker each morning. Sarah felt smothered and didn't know what to do. She eventually decided to confront Barbie about her need to make other friends and to decide how to handle some situations on her own. When Sarah confronted Barbie, she emphasized her good points, the qualities that would attract friends to her, and her growing abilities in decision making. Barbie was better able to change her actions by building on her strengths instead of fighting her weaknesses.

Not only do two friends confront each other about harmful actions; they sometimes simply get angry with each other. At times people feel bad and are more touchy than usual. Anger and frustration are inevitable in a close friendship. We are better off dealing with our differences, instead of shying away from them and allowing them to build up to a later explosion.

Arguments can be handled in both good and bad ways. By learn-

ing some tips on how to disagree, we can help our friendships grow stronger, rather than fall apart through arguments. **We need to talk to our friends about how we feel, not about what is wrong with them.** We place people on the defensive when we attack them for something they have done.

We should discuss only one topic at a time, instead of dragging past disagreements or a whole list of complaints into the conversation. We should be able to express any complaint in one sentence.

Our criticism should be balanced with expressions of love. We may react angrily to something our friends say or do, but we should then concentrate on saying caring words. This will show them that our anger does not cancel out the love in our friendship. When our friends become angry with us, we should remind ourselves that their anger does not erase their love for us. A person can feel both love and anger at the same time.

We should apologize when we are wrong. We may misjudge our friends and jump to wrong conclusions, or we may take out our hurt and anger on friends who just happen to be around at the time. In such cases we should apologize quickly and offer an explanation. We all make mistakes at times. Offering an apology does not prove we are weak. It shows that we are strong enough to admit we are human.

Arguments need not have winners. In fact, arguments should not have winners. We often hear the question, Who won the argument? but the real purpose of our disagreements should be to clear the air.

Our friends should have an opportunity to state their side in any argument. It is unfair for us to blow up at our friends, then storm away. Ending an argument by slamming the door on our way out only weakens a relationship.

We can take the initiative in forgiving, allowing flaws in another just as we do in ourselves. Alan Loy McGinnis says in his book *The Friendship Factor,*

> We tend to see ourselves not for what we are but for what we strive to be, whereas we see others for what they are. Jesus, in his encounters with people such as Peter and the woman at the well, saw them for what they were trying to become and what they could be. To extend such understanding toward our intimates can do a great deal to build strong friendships.[4]

We are responsible for checking our own attitudes, not those of our friends, as we forgive them.

When friends become angry with us, we need not panic. Their anger probably does not mean that the friendship is over. If we respond to their anger by getting mad ourselves, we should express that anger. We can then work through our differences in a positive way.

Sometimes we will need to find a way to get rid of our anger rather than expressing it directly to our friends. They may be dealing with a major problem or depending on us to help them feel good about themselves. For example, a friend might do something to make us angry while he is experiencing grief over the death of his father. He has too much stress at that point to handle a disagreement with us. We need to find another way to vent our anger. Expressing our angry feelings to someone we trust, such as our mother, our Sunday School teacher, or another friend, is one way of unleashing our anger. We may need to use this approach when we get mad at a teacher, coach, principal, or some other adult with authority over us.

Doing something active, such as running, swimming, or cleaning our room, may help us get rid of our angry feelings. If we get very angry or hostile, we should release our aggression in some way before discussing our feelings with our friend. We will then be able to keep calm and have a positive discussion.[5]

Since no two people are exactly alike, disagreements and misunderstandings will come up between friends. The way we handle our differences will help determine whether we grow closer or farther apart.

> "If you become angry, do not let
> your anger lead you into sin, and
> do not stay angry all day."
> Ephesians 4:26 (TEV)

[1]Gary Collins, How to Be a People Helper (Santa Ana, California: Vision House Publishers, 1976), p. 50.
[2]David W. Johnson, Reaching Out (Englewood Cliffs, New Jersey: Prentice-Hall, Inc., 1972), p. 160.
[3]Ibid., p. 162.
[4]Alan Loy McGinnis, The Friendship Factor (Minneapolis: Augsburg Publishing House, 1979). p. 160.
[5]Ibid., pp. 136-7.

Chapter 8

Friends in Crisis

"Larry and his father were very close. They swam, played tennis, and spent time talking about life. Last week Larry's father fell dead in his office with a massive heart attack. I went to the funeral, and I went by the house to see Larry the next day. He seemed so numb. It was like he was in another world. He came back to school yesterday, but he's really out of it. A lot of people just sort of avoid really talking to him at all. I know that's not right, but it's hard to know what to say. I'm his friend, and it hurts to see him like this."

"I have a friend who was raped last summer. Since then she has become very withdrawn and nervous. She still has terrible nightmares about the incident, but she is ashamed to go to any adult for help. Recently she has expressed that she just doesn't want to live anymore. She says that death would be a lot better than living with the nightmares and the shame. She wouldn't really kill herself, would she? What can I do to stop her? I feel like I'm sitting by helplessly waiting for her to destroy herself."

Sometimes our friends face problems that are overwhelming. We call these problems crises. A crisis is a problem that is so major that nothing else in that person's life matters until it is dealt with. It is a situation that cannot wait until later. Something must be done immediately.

67

Some problems we can easily identify as crises. When a friend is raped, she is experiencing a crisis. The death of a parent, a drug overdose, and a suicide threat are obvious crises. Yet we cannot always decide whether a friend is going through a crisis just by knowing the nature of the problem. Finding out that one's parents are getting a divorce, failing a grade in school, and breaking up with one's boyfriend may be crises for some people, but less urgent problems for others. We can determine whether or not specific problems are crises for our friends by learning to watch for some clues in their actions.

A friend going through a crisis may not seem to be listening to us. People in crisis situations often have difficulty concentrating on any single thought. We need to be careful not to become frustrated or angry because they are not paying attention. Rather, we should seek to understand the reason for their lack of attention.

Friends in crises may avoid looking at us. They may sit and stare at the floor, or they may appear to stare through whatever they are looking at. In any case, they are not able to look us in the eye. When they are using all their powers of thought to decide on a way out of a crisis, they do not think about what their eyes are seeing. They only think about the problem.

Friends experiencing crises may behave in ways that are unusual for them. Loud persons may suddenly become very quiet, or quiet persons may become very loud. We will notice when persons close to us are acting unusual. A stranger may never suspect that anything is wrong, but we can tell that our friends are not their usual selves.

Friends in crisis may suddenly not be able to get along with their family or friends. When people are under extreme stress, they may not be able to show love. They may begin to treat people close to them very badly.

Another sign of crisis is an inability to get any work done. Our friends' grades may begin dropping drastically, or they may stop turning in their assignments at school.[1]

We can be sensitive to the possibility of a crisis when friends

are going through a potentially upsetting experience. Their parents may tell them that the family is moving to another town, or they may suspect their parents are planning to get a divorce. Our friends may or may not respond to these situations as to a crisis, but we can be alert to their reactions in case they do.

In times of crisis our friends may outwardly reveal their inner turmoil by not eating, crying easily, not caring about their appearance, not having much energy, or not being able to sleep.

None of these clues, taken alone, necessarily means that our friends are going through a crisis. However, they can help us recognize the possible seriousness of the problem and the need for immediate help. There are several basic things we can do to help our friends through a crisis.

The most important way we can help is to be with them. We may have had other plans, but when we recognize friends in crisis, our priority is to give our time to them. We cannot understand their pain and confusion if we have not experienced what they are going through. This may cause frustration for us. In such cases, we might say something like, "I've never gone through what you are feeling right now. But I have hurt before, and I want you to know that, as much as I can, I'm feeling with you right now." The word *with* is an important word for us to use because it lessens the loneliness our friends may feel in dealing with their crises. We should not say, "I know how you feel." We may have gone through a similar experience, but we are different people, and we do not know how they feel.

We should expect to be able to help our friends through a crisis. We can communicate confidence through speaking firmly, but gently, with a calm, slow voice. Friends who feel hopeless in dealing with their problems may gain new strength through the hope they sense in our voice and attitude.

Touching our friends may help them understand that we care and that we are with them both physically and emotionally. A hug or a hand on the arm may help to bring them more firmly into a sense of the present, and it may enable them to release some of 69 their pent-up emotions. We can get in touch with friends by looking them in the eyes and helping them to look back at us. We may then be able to communicate a calming hope more directly.

We should not feel the need to leap to solutions, but we should walk with our hurting friends through their emotions. They may then arrive at a solution, or they may simply need someone to listen and care while they hurt and grieve. When we must leave our friends who are experiencing crises, we should be sure that someone else is with them. For example, we might stay with them in their home until their parents or other family members arrive.

Sometimes friends in crisis will need help beyond what we can offer. When that happens, we should help them find the person or agency that can offer additional help. Seeking outside help does not mean that we have failed. It means that we are wise enough to recognize our limitations.

We should look to outside help when we are not getting anywhere in helping our friends. If they are severely depressed or suicidal or need medical attention, we must seek professional help for them. Friends with legal or financial difficulties need advice from someone with more knowledge in those areas than we have. If we find ourselves disliking the person we are helping, someone else probably would be of more help.

We can begin now to think about who might be of the most help to our friends when they have special needs. We will then be ready to offer suggestions when a crisis suddenly arises.

A good starting point in seeking outside help for another is to think about who we would go to if we needed help. Our pastor, youth director, school counselor, a teacher, a doctor, or an adult friend could offer help or suggest places to go for help.

The next step could be to check the phone book for agencies or organizations that offer help, such as mental health associations and clinics, Alcoholics Anonymous or Alateen groups, legal aid societies and lawyers, medical doctors, welfare agencies, and telephone crisis lines. We should know the phone number to call in case of an emergency requiring an ambulance, police, or the fire department. If we are not certain what kind of help an organization offers, we can call and ask. For example, a phone call to

70

Alcoholics Anonymous may tell us what kind of help is available for teenage alcoholics or teenagers with alcoholic parents.

When we decide to suggest our friends seek outside help, we should honestly discuss the need with them. We can then decide together who would be of most help. Our friends may need to know that most professional counselors, including pastors, doctors, and lawyers, are bound by a code of ethics to keep all conversations in confidence. They may still want to ask them if everything they say will be private. If there is a cost for professional help, we may find out about it in advance.

We should not abandon our friends when they seek outside help. They need to know of our continuing friendship and support. If they talk with a professional counselor, we can ask how they felt about the visit, but not what was actually said.

Our friends should tell their parents when they seek outside help. In many places, such as the emergency room of a hospital,

their consent will be needed before help can be offered. In certain exceptional situations, our friends may feel they should not or cannot tell their parents about the help they are receiving. They should seek the advice of the professional counselor or a wise adult friend before definitely deciding not to tell their parents.

We may have a friend facing a serious crisis who is considering suicide. We need to be aware of some serious signs which could indicate a person is suicidal. Persons considering suicide may do and say things which show us they feel a great deal of hate toward themselves. They may call themselves stupid, they may drink more or take stronger drugs, or they may drive recklessly.

Another indication of the possibility of suicide is a constant appearance of being nervous or shook-up. This may include rapid breathing, dizziness, and other signs of obvious anxiety.

Persons considering suicide may talk as if there is only one way out of a crisis. In reality there may be many ways out, but suicide is the only solution they can talk about. They may tend to use words such as *forever, never,* or *always* if they have reached this stage. If they talk about ways they might kill themselves, we should be especially alerted to the seriousness of their state of mind.[2] The idea that persons who talk about suicide will not actually do it is false. Their words are to be taken very seriously. Another clue is their speaking of their actions with an air of finality. They might say, "This is the last test I will ever take."

Persons who have shown some signs of considering suicide may have been very tense, then suddenly become relaxed. Their moment of relaxation may be the moment of decision to commit suicide. We may be falsely encouraged that they are no longer tense, when in fact their relaxation is a serious reason for concern.[3]

We can take several steps to help friends who are considering suicide. **We can agree with them that their problems are real.** We can try to understand how they are feeling. This will help them know that someone cares.

Our next step is to listen carefully and intently. We should talk calmly and slowly, thereby helping to reduce the high pitch of emotion and tension which they feel. Hopefully, they will gain strength from us and feel less frantic. Persons who are in the beginning stages of considering suicide may respond positively to talk about the effects of their suicide on people they love. If they are in the later and more serious stages, we can talk about things that matter to them or a dream they have not yet accomplished. We should try to help them discover a reason for living.[4]

It is dangerous to try to shock depressed persons by telling them to go ahead and kill themselves. We may feel impatient and frustrated with their threats, but suicide is too serious for this approach. We should not argue with them over whether it is better to live or die. The belief that it is better to live should be our absolute assumption which cannot be questioned.

Persons who are threatening suicide must not be left alone. We should stay with them or make certain that someone who is going to be with them knows of their threats.

It is essential that persons threatening suicide receive outside help. They need to talk to someone who has experience in helping people handle the kinds of problems that have driven them to consider suicide.

Persons who have attempted suicide or who have been in a mental hospital may feel uncomfortable when they return to school and see their old friends. We can show our willingness to continue our friendship by inviting them to our home or asking them to do something with us. We can include them in group activities as they feel ready for them. We must not push them to discuss their suicide attempt or hospital stay. We must be careful to avoid being overly curious about their experiences. The best thing we can do is to take positive steps toward reestablishing our friendship.

Our parents may naturally be concerned when we reach out to persons who have had serious problems, such as suicide attempts, drug addiction, or criminal records. We should respect their concerns and make an extra effort to tell them as much as possible about our friends without breaking any confidences. We can invite our friends to our home so our parents can meet them. Our parents may help us see some possible dangers in a relationship   73 and show us how to protect ourselves from harm or involvement in questionable activities.

Another crisis in which our friends will need help is the death of someone close to them, perhaps a member of their family or a friend. Consider Larry, whose father died suddenly from a heart attack. The most helpful thing we can do for Larry is simply to be with him after the death. Our presence says that we care, even when we cannot think of any words to say. We can go to his house and express our sorrow over his father's death. Then we need to let Larry talk about whatever he wishes. If he becomes emotional, we should not try to quiet him. We should just listen. If we knew his father, we can talk about our good memories of him. If Larry does not want to talk at that time, we should keep our visit short. Before we leave we need to be sure that Larry knows we will be around if he needs us.

Above all, we should not ignore the death and avoid talking to Larry about it. We should not deny the reality of death by telling him that everything will be all right. Larry may be experiencing

shock or denial of death himself—the first stage of grief. He may have trouble believing his father is really dead, and he may feel numb at times. When he visits the funeral home or goes to the funeral service, he may begin to face the reality of death, as painful as it might be.

The second stage of grief is anger—toward God, the person who has died, the family, or you as a friend. Larry may be angry at people who are not hurting in the same way he is. He may feel guilty that he didn't show more love or do something to prevent the death. If Larry had an argument with his father the morning of his death, he may feel additional guilt that their last words were cross ones. He may even be afraid that the argument upset his father and somehow contributed to his death.

During this period of anger, we need to accept Larry's moods. We do not have to give him an answer for why his father died. We can listen to his expressions of anger and fear and perhaps find outside help for him if he carries an especially heavy load of guilt.

The third stage of grief is usually depression. During this stage Larry may have trouble eating and sleeping. The reality of death is sinking in. The fourth stage is acceptance—the period in which Larry decides he must adjust to the death and go on living.[5]

Every person is an individual and faces death in his own way. All people do not go through each of the four stages of grief, and they do not express anger or guilt in the same ways. We can rely on what we know of our friends' usual reactions in order to know when they are hurting and need to know that we care.

During the period immediately after a death, we can make specific offers to help, rather than saying, "Is there anything I can do?" We might deliver messages to a teacher, friend, or coach or pick up homework assignments. We can run errands, such as taking clothes to the cleaners or buying a bottle of shampoo. We can help straighten up the house, since other people will be coming to visit. We can help care for small children, help cook food for the family, or help keep a record of food that other people bring. Our friend will also appreciate our going to the funeral home or to the funeral service.

After the funeral when our friend has returned to school, we can make an extra effort to do things together, such as going to a movie or football game. It is important for a person experiencing

75

grief to get back into a normal routine of school and social activities as soon as possible. This may also be a good time to share our faith in Christ if our friend is not a Christian.

Our commitment to help friends who are experiencing grief will need to continue long after the actual death and funeral. They may have the greatest need to talk six months or even a year after the death. We should continue our sensitivity to their feelings so that they will feel free to talk about their grief whenever they are ready to do so.

When a person we do not know well returns to school after a death, we can say we were sorry to hear what happened. We do not have to use flowery words to show we care. We might also send a card to that person when we hear about the death.

Periods of crisis for our friends may be frightening to us as we wonder what we should say or do. Yet periods of crisis may be the best opportunities to witness of Christ. First we show Christ's love as we stick by our friends through the hard times. Then we can speak of Christ's power to heal. Where there is intense hurt and pain, there is a greater need for us to commit ourselves to care.

> *"There is a friend who sticks*
> *closer than a brother."*
> Proverbs 18:24

[1]*Paul Welter*, How to Help a Friend (*Wheaton, Illinois: Tyndale House Publishers, Inc., 1978*), *pp.* 67-8.
[2]*Ibid., pp.* 278-80.
[3]*Gary Collins*, How to Be a People Helper (*Santa Ana, California: Vision House Publishers, 1976*), *p.* 103.
[4]*Welter*, How to Help a Friend, *pp.* 281-2.
[5]*Dianna Daniels Booher*, The Faces of Death (*Nashville: Broadman Press, 1980*), *pp*, 37-40.

Chapter 9

When We Need Help

"*My friends are very important to me. When they have problems, I hurt with them, and I'm learning real ways to help them. Sometimes I find ways to tell them about Christ too. I'm working hard at being a real friend, and some days I think I'm doing all right. But sometimes I wonder if I'm doing any good at all. Sometimes my friends don't accept my help, or their problems don't work out like I think they should. I get discouraged, and then I get lonely, and I wonder if anybody knows how I really feel. Sometimes life hurts—even when you're on the helping side.*"

A Friend

When we accept the responsibility of helping others, we will at times feel inadequate, frustrated, and physically and emotionally tired. We need to know where to get strength, wisdom, and help for ourselves.

A daily quiet time with God will provide a foundation from which we can reach out and help others. We must know God before we can help others know him. The love we receive from him leads us to spread the good news of Christ and to share his love with others. As we read the Bible, we will grow in our understanding of people, their needs, and ways we can help.

We should have our quiet time at the same time and place every   79 day if possible. This will help us establish a regular schedule of Bible reading and prayer. We can talk to God about our own needs and the needs of people we are helping. God promises to help when we do not know which direction to turn in meeting a need. James 1:5 (TEV) says, "If any of you lack wisdom, he should pray to God, who will give it to him; because God gives generously and graciously to all." We are also told in 1 Peter 5:7 to turn our worries and concerns over to God, who loves and cares for us. We do not have to meet our friends' needs by ourselves. Through prayer we trust God to lead us to know people we can help, to recognize opportunities to minister, and to know the words to say and the things to do in order to help.

Another part of our daily prayer life is a dependence on God to forgive us and to show us the parts of our own lives that need change and growth. Our prayer can be that of the psalmist in Psalm 139:23-24. "Search me, O God, and know my heart; try me and know my anxious thoughts; And see if there be any hurtful way in me, and lead me in everlasting way." Our aim is to have the personal qualities which are most like Christ. The description of a Christlike personality is found in Galatians 5:22-23: "The fruit of the Spirit is love, joy, peace, patience, kindness, goodness, faithfulness, gentleness, self-control."

The evidence that Christ is the center of our lives will show in our thoughts, feelings, and actions. He will help us choose the books we read, the movies we watch, the music we listen to, and the activities in which we spend much of our time. The things we hear and think about regularly will begin to dominate our thoughts. Philippians 4:8 (TEV) tells us, "Fill your minds with those things that are good and that deserve praise: things that are true, noble, right, pure, lovely, and honorable."

We will be able to help other people grow and make the best choices only if we are growing and looking to Christ for the choices and decisions we make. Any sin in our lives will slow our growth and threaten our ability to help other people. When we argue with our brothers and sisters, have an attitude of superiority, or think lustful thoughts, we hurt both ourselves and any people we might have helped. We cannot sin in one area of our lives without it affecting all other areas.

On the other hand, we must not be defeated when we realize we have sinned. God promises to forgive us when we ask him. Through our mistakes we can learn how to help a friend who later makes a similar mistake.

Through a close relationship with God, we can learn to accept ourselves with both our strengths and weaknesses. God has placed a high value on us by creating us in his image. We become his sons and daughters through faith in Christ. God gives us personalities and abilities which are uniquely our own. We are freed from having to try to match the skills of someone else. We are called to use our unique abilities to their fullest to reach out to people to whom God leads us. We feel better about ourselves when we become involved in his work of helping others.

We also need a human friend who will help and guide us. Of course, we need friends who are near our own age. We also need an adult friend who will affirm us, offer advice, and warn us when our helping actions may cause us harm. This special friend should have:
1. a growing Christian faith
2. a willingness to seek God's guidance in all decisions
3. wisdom and maturity
4. an understanding of the teenager's world
5. ability to keep a confidence
6. honesty and directness.

We should trust this friend enough to admit our needs and limitations. The willingness to admit our needs to another person is a strength, not a weakness, for we are then able to face our problems squarely. Finally, praying together can strengthen our relationship. We can take needs and problems to God with the promise that "if two of you agree on earth about anything that they may ask, it shall be done for them by My Father who is in heaven" (Matt. 18:19).

We also receive help from the friends we are helping. They may lead us to examine our values more closely, teach us through their strengths, and offer us love and affirmation. When we are most effective in giving love to our friends, we will be most open to receiving love. We cannot expect friends to accept our offer of caring and refuse their caring in return.

Sometimes we will be hurt or feel defeated in the process of helping others. It is important for us to have a support group of Christian friends committed to helping others. That support group may be found at church or among our Christian friends at school. We may pray and study the Bible together and offer encouragement to each other. We can share our excitement and help each other through inevitable discouragements.

During prayertimes we can share the needs we have discovered. We may have prayer partners within our group and commit ourselves to pray for each other daily. However, we must be careful not to break any confidences during prayer. Our prayer requests should never sink to the level of gossip lists.

The Great Commission in Matthew 28:19-20 expresses our purpose as Christians: "Go therefore and make disciples of all the nations, baptizing them in the name of the Father and the Son and the Holy Spirit, teaching them to observe all that I commanded you; and lo, I am with you always, even to the end of the age." Our actions toward our friends should witness to the power of Jesus in our lives and cause them to seek him.

We accept great challenges and responsibilities in being someone's friend. To become like Christ is to dare to minister to people in ways of which we never believed ourselves to be capable. We will have our low points and frustrations, but our rewards will come as we lead people toward God's choices and plans for their lives.

> *"I have called you friends, for all*
> *things that I have heard from*
> *My Father I have made known*
> *to you."*
> *John 15:15*

Learning Activities

Chapter 1

1. Begin a journal in which you will keep a record of the things you are learning about helping and the ways you are growing as a friend. List your personal qualities that will be helpful. What are your greatest strengths? Write down some ways you can use your strengths to help other people.

2. In your journal, list two or three friends who have helped you. What are some of their characteristics that make them good friends?

3. Look up some Bible verses and discuss what they teach us about ways we can help other people: Zechariah 7:9; Matthew 18:15; Luke 17:3-4; John 13:35; Romans 12:15; 1 Corinthians 8:9-13; 1 John 3:17-18.

4. In your journal, list some concerns or problems you have that you fear might keep you from being a real friend. Put an X by the concerns you cannot discuss with anyone and a + by the concerns you can discuss with someone you trust.

Some possible concerns you might list are:

a) I am so shy that I have trouble making new friends or talking to people.

b) When someone disagrees with me or is angry with me, my feelings are easily hurt.

c) I'm a Christian, but I don't make time to read my Bible or pray regularly. I may try for a few days, but then I forget and can't get back in the habit.

d) I want people to like me so much that I'm afraid to disagree or stand up to them.

e) I tend to be critical and only see the faults in others.

Discuss how these barriers could be overcome.[1]

Chapter 2

1. Why do you want to be a friend? Consider both good and bad reasons you may have for helping other people. Write your answers in your journal.

2. You will need a box of tinker toys for this activity, which will demonstrate the best type of helping relationship. Ask three volunteers to leave the room. Next, ask three people from the remaining group to serve as builder's helpers. Explain that they will be acting out three different styles of helping: a) taking over for the person we are helping; b) being present, but offering almost no help; and c) helping the person solve his own problem.

Each builder's helper is handed a card describing that type of helping role. Each one is to read and act out the role, but not tell anyone what the card says. The cards should read as follows:

a) I am an expert. In order to make sure that you build a good tower, I am going to show you how.

b) I don't want to be rude and get in your way, so you just go ahead and build the tower yourself. I will watch you, but I don't really care how you go about building it.

c) I am confident that you can build a good tower. I want to help, so please let me know if there is any way I can assist in solving the problem.

Call the first volunteer back into the room. Say "You have four minutes to build a tower out of tinker toys. You will be assisted by one of the builder's helpers." Ask the group to be aware of their own feelings and the way the builder and helper relate to each other. Tell them to notice ways the helper is or is not being helpful to the builder.

When the first builder's time is up, bring in the second builder, then the third. After all three builders have finished, ask the group to decide which style of helping was best. Ask the builders and helpers how they felt about their roles. Ask the entire group how the principle demonstrated in this activity can be applied to helping relationships with friends.[2]

3. Answer the following true-false questions.

____a) Skilled professional counselors are always able to help more than a friend who has little training or experience.

____b) A good helping relationship is a two-way street; both people help each other.

____c) Most people tend to react to problems in the same way.

____d) We should always be able to supply an answer for the problems our friends are having.

____e) A person must desire to change or want help in order for a friend to be of any real assistance.

____f) A good beginning point in helping a friend is often to discover the values that you share.

____g) A friend should not be required to change his actions and attitudes in order to continue a friendship with us.

[Key: a) False; b) True; c) False; d) False; e) True; f) True; g) True]

Chapter 3

1. In your journal, list three people you would like to befriend. What are some ways you can get to know them better? Write down what you will do this week to show them you would like to be their friend.

2. Practice affirming friends by affirming the people who are studying this book with you. Choose one person in the group. Ask the rest of the group to name that person's strengths and positive qualities. The person being affirmed cannot respond verbally. After one person has been affirmed, go on to the next until everyone in the group has had a turn.

3. Divide into groups of two. Read the following situations, one at a time. Ask one person in the pair to tell how to offer friendship in each situation.

a) You are sitting at a football game with several of your friends. A person sitting nearby is making insulting and hateful remarks to the people he is with. They finally get mad and walk off, leaving him sitting alone. You go up to talk to him, but he says something obnoxious to you.

b) A group of students are standing in front of their lockers talking. A girl they consider strange and different walks up and

acts as if she wants to join them. They ignore her until someone finally says, "Why don't you just get lost?" She drops her
head and walks away.

c) You are sitting in class waiting for the teacher to come in.
   Several students are making fun of one of the other students.
   He doesn't say anything, but he looks at you as though he
   wants you to do something.

d) A new girl in school is constantly talking about how much
   better her old school was. She puts down the students at
   your school and praises her friends from the previous school.
   One afternoon you meet her as you are walking out the
   school door.[3]

Chapter 4

1. Trust games can help members of a group learn to trust and
respect each other. They can be used as discussion starters for
considering our feelings about trusting others. Individuals in the
group should not be pressured to participate, and no one should
participate who is not willing to act in a trustworthy manner. The
games must be followed by discussion in order to be helpful as
teaching tools.

a) Circle Game—Six to ten people form a circle and stand
   with their arms extended toward the center. One blindfolded
   person stands in the center, relaxes, and falls back into the
   arms of the circle.

b) Trust Walk—The people in the group are divided into pairs.
   One person in each couple is blindfolded. The other person
   leads the blindfolded one on a walk. The leader guides the
   blindfolded person to feel various objects. After about 15
   minutes, the members of the pairs trade roles.

c) People Lift—A group of at least six people stand facing each
   other in a double line, while one blindfolded person lies face
   up between the lines. The group lifts this person high over
   their heads.

2. You will need scissors and different-colored sheets of construction paper for this activity. Ask members of the group to
choose construction paper and cut or fold it into shapes that represent their personalities. Participants should then explain their
creations.

3. In order for members of the group to gain experience in   87

openness, trust, and risk taking, have them stand up, mill around the room, and greet each person without using any words. They may wink, shake hands, smile, or use other gestures. Members of the group should then choose as a partner the person they know least well. For five minutes (2½ minutes each), they should take turns describing one of their daydreams: becoming President of the United States, scoring the winning bucket in a basketball game, etc.

The group should change partners, take one minute to complete one of the following sentences, then move to a different partner for each sentence.

a) The animal I would most like to be and the reason . . .
b) The quality I like most in myself is . . .
c) If I could change one thing about myself . . .
d) The song that means the most to me and the reason . . .
e) The ways in which we are similar or different are . . .

Have the group discuss their thoughts and feeling about opening themselves to others.[4]

Chapter 5

1. Write the names of a variety of emotions and feelings (nervous, happy, hurt, bored, angry, confident, loved, jealous) on sheets of paper. One at a time, have members of the group draw a slip of paper and act out their assigned emotion without using any words. The rest of the group should guess the emotion.

2. Practice showing warmth, both verbally and nonverbally, in response to the following statements.

a) I hate to go home anymore. My parents are always arguing and don't seem to notice when I am around. I just don't know what to do.

b) There is no way I can get everything done. I have two tests next week, an essay to write, and my job at the florist shop. Now Mr. Marshall says we must have extra band rehearsals. I wish everyone would leave me alone.

c) I don't know why Brenda got so mad at me. I only went out with Brad when I thought she didn't like him anymore. But now she just ignores me. She won't believe me when I try to explain. I thought she was my friend.

3. Evaluate your abilities as a good listener by filling out the following chart.[5] Keep the chart in your journal.

a) I believe that listening to others is a very important way to help them. □Never □Sometimes □Usually
b) Others would say that I am "quick to hear and slow to speak." □Never □Sometimes □Usually
c) I interrupt other people when they are talking. □Never □Sometimes □Usually
d) When others are talking, I am thinking about what I am going to say next. □Never □Sometimes □Usually
e) I look people in the eye when they talk to me. □Never □Sometimes □Usually

I could be a better listener if I _____

Two people who would say that I am a sensitive listener are _____ and _____.

Chapter 6

1. In your journal, write the names of one or two people who may need you as a friend. What are some ways you can help them? Develop a plan for helping, and keep a record of the things you actually do. You may want to make a copy of pages 90-91 and write in answers to the questions. If you have a *DiscipleYouth* notebook,[6] put this worksheet behind the Discipling tab. This will give you a way to look back and measure the progress that you and your friend have made.

What are some ways you seek help for yourself when you have a problem? Have you learned any other possibilities from this chapter?

2. Using wire, string, and construction paper, make a mobile showing different ways of helping people. For example, you might cut a leaf out of construction paper to represent the help found in nature, or you might shape an eighth note from wire to represent music.

3. Write a note to a friend. In the note affirm that person's positive qualities.

4. Complete an acrostic by suggesting possible ways to help friends with different kinds of needs (new Christian, drugs, can't make friends, moving, new at school, lonely, blind). For example:

S tart conversation with him to make it easier to talk. _____

H _____

Y _____

"Let us not love with words or tongue but with actions and in truth" 1 John 3:18 (NIV).	FRIENDS ARE FOR HELPING

A personal plan to help my friend . . .
NAME: DATE:

Is this friend a Christian?   ☐Yes   ☐No   ☐Not sure

NEEDS OR PROBLEMS FACING MY FRIEND:

WAYS OF HELPING MY FRIEND:

IS THERE SOMEONE I SHOULD TALK TO ABOUT THIS?

NOTES ON RESPONSES AND ANSWERS TO PRAYER:

DATE	ENTRY

91

Chapter 7

1. Think about a conflict you have had in the past. Describe it in your journal. List the ways you handled the conflict. What were some helpful things each party in the conflict did? What could you have done better?

2. Write down the responses you would make to the following situations that call for a confrontation.

   a) I don't see why you can't go ahead and have a drink like the rest of us. How do you think it makes the rest of us feel when we are sitting here with our beers and you are holding a soft drink?

   b) Why don't you and your church friends just back off? My taking drugs doesn't hurt you.

   c) Hey, I thought you liked me and were enjoying our date. Why don't you loosen up a little bit and prove it?

3. Divide into groups of three, and have each person in the triad contribute 25 cents. Place the 75 cents in the middle of each group of three.

Each group has 15 minutes to decide how to divide the money. Only two people may receive any money. It is not fair to flip a coin to see who gets it. The object of the game is for each person to get as much money as possible.

After the activity is completed, have group members describe their feelings and examine the ways they handled a potential conflict. Discuss different ways people handle conflicts and how you can reduce the tension in arguments.[7]

4. Think of a topic about which there is or could be disagreement within the group. Divide the large group into two smaller groups, and assign each group an opposing point of view. Allow 15 minutes for the groups to prepare arguments for their sides.

Pair up the group with one member of each couple representing each of the two points of view. Designate members of the pair as A and B. Person A is allowed five minutes to express that group's point of view, then person B speaks for two minutes supporting A's point of view.

Person B speaks next for five minutes explaining that group's side of the argument. Person A speaks for two minutes supporting B's point of view.

Persons A and B are given five minutes to come up with a joint agreement on the issue they are discussing. They must follow one rule: Before responding to another's statement, each must re-express what that person has just said. Ask the whole group to discuss whether taking the other person's point of view helped in reaching an agreement.[8]

Chapter 8

1. Prepare a card file on people and agencies in your area to whom you might refer friends you are helping. On each card include the name, phone number, hours, cost, and types of help available.

2. Plan a field trip to visit an agency or hospital to learn about the types of help offered. Arrange for someone who works there to give a tour and talk about the ways they help.

3. Invite your pastor to talk to the group studying this book about how to help persons who are either facing their own death or grieving over the death of someone they love.

4. What are some of the experiences you have had with grief? How did you feel, and what did people do or say that helped you the most? How have you helped others who were grieving? What ways of helping have you observed? Write your thoughts in your journal.

Chapter 9

1. Look up some Bible verses and discuss what they say about the ways God helps us: Psalm 46:1; Proverbs 3:5-6; Isaiah 40:31; John 14:26; Philippians 4:19; Hebrews 4:16; Hebrews 13:6.

2. In your journal, list some sources of help available to you. Who is a special adult friend of yours? Who are some special friends your own age? Do you have a support group at your church or school? Do you have a prayer partner? If not, can you think of someone you might ask to pray with you?

3. Rate yourself on a scale of one to five for different aspects of the Christian personality as found in Galatians 5:22-23.

a) Love   Very Low 1 : 2 : 3 : 4 : 5 Very High
b) Joy   Very Low 1 : 2 : 3 : 4 : 5 Very High
c) Peace   Very Low 1 : 2 : 3 : 4 : 5 Very High
d) Patience   Very Low 1 : 2 : 3 : 4 : 5 Very High
e) Kindness   Very Low 1 : 2 : 3 : 4 : 5 Very High
f) Goodness   Very Low 1 : 2 : 3 : 4 : 5 Very High
g) Faithfulness   Very Low 1 : 2 : 3 : 4 : 5 Very High
h) Gentleness   Very Low 1 : 2 : 3 : 4 : 5 Very High
i) Self-control   Very Low 1 : 2 : 3 : 4 : 5 Very High

4. If you do not have a daily quiet time, begin one. You will find help in *DiscipleYouth Notebook*, Sessions 3 and 4,[9] and *Survival Kit for New Christians*, Youth Edition.[10]

Write in your journal ways you can use your strengths to help people and ways you can improve on your weaknesses.

[1]*Gary Collins*, People Helper Growthbook (*Santa Ana, California: Vision House Publishers, 1976*), *pp.* 30-32.

[2]*Mimi and Don Samuels*, The Complete Handbook of Peer Counseling (*Miami: Fiesta Publishing Corp., 1974*), *pp.* 96-8.

[3]*David W. Johnson*, Reaching Out (*Englewood Cliffs, New Jersey: Prentice-Hall, Inc., 1972*), *p.* 31.

[4]*Ibid., pp.* 19-20.

[5]*Norman Wakefield*, Listening: A Christian's Guide to Loving Relationships (*Waco: Word Books, 1981*), *pp.* 20-21.

[6]*Clyde R. Hall, Jr., and Joe L. Ford (comp.)*, DiscipleYouth Notebook (*Nashville: Convention Press, 1982*). DiscipleYouth Notebook *is part of* Disciple-Youth Kit *available from Material Services Department, Sunday School Board, 127 Ninth Avenue North, Nashville, TN 37234 $16.95.*

[7]*Johnson*, Reaching Out, *pp.* 206-7.

[8]*Johnson, pp.* 214-15.

[9]*Clyde R. Hall, Jr., and Joe L. Ford (comps.)*, DiscipleYouth Notebook (*Nashville: Convention Press, 1982*).

[10]*Ralph W. Neighbour, Jr.*, Survival Kit for New Christians, *Youth Edition* (*Nashville: Convention Press, 1981*).

For Further Reading

Arnold, William V. *When Your Parents Divorce*. Philadelphia: The Westminister Press, 1980.

Booher, Dianna Daniels. *The Faces of Death*. Nashville: Broadman Press, 1980.

Coleman, Lucien. *Training Youth to Witness Kit*. Birmingham: Woman's Missionary Union, 1977.

Collins, Gary. *How to Be a People Helper*. Santa Ana, California: Vision House Publishers, 1976.

Drakeford, John W. *A Christian View of Homosexuality*. Nashville: Broadman Press, 1977.

Hall, R. Clyde, Jr., and Ford, Joe L. *DiscipleYouth Notebook*. Nashville: Convention Press, 1982.

Hearn, Janice W. *Making Friends, Keeping Friends*. Garden City, New York: Doubleday and Company, Inc., 1979.

Johnson, David W. *Reaching Out*. Englewood Cliffs, New Jersey: Prentice-Hall, Inc., 1972.

Kennedy, Eugene. *Crisis Counseling*. New York: Continuum Publishing Corporation, 1981.

Klagsbrun, Francine. *Too Young to Die: Youth and Suicide*. New York: Pocket Books, 1976.

Little, Paul E. *How to Give Away Your Faith*. Illinois: InterVarsity Press, 1966.

McDill, Wayne. *Making Friends for Chirst*. Nashville: Broadman Press, 1980.

McGinnis, Alan Loy. *The Friendship Factor*. Minneapolis: Augsburg Publishing House, 1979.

Monfalcone, Wesley R. *Coping with Abuse in the Family*. Philadelphia: The Westminister Press, 1980.

Murphree, T. Garvice, and Murphree, Dorothy. *Understanding Youth*. Nashville: Convention Press, 1969.

Narramore, Bruce. *You're Someone Special*. Grand Rapids, Michigan: Zondervan Publishing House, 1978.

Neighbour, Ralph W., Jr. *Survival Kit for New Christians*, Youth Edition. Nashville: Convention Press, 1981.

Richards, Arlene, and Willis, Irene. *How to Get It Together When Your Parents Are Coming Apart*. New York: Bantam Books, 1976.

Schmidt, Paul. *Coping with Difficult People*. Philadelphia: The Westminister Press, 1980.

Strommen, Merton P. *Five Cries of Youth*. New York: Harper and Row Publishers, Inc., 1974.

Wakefield, Norman. *Listening: A Christian's Guide to Loving Relationships*. Waco: Word Books, 1981.

Welter, Paul. *How to Help a Friend*. Wheaton, Illinois: Tyndale House Publishers, Inc., 1978.